Trademark Acknowledgments

Wrox has endeavored to provide trademark information about all the companies and products mentioned in this book by the appropriate use of capitals. However, Wrox cannot guarantee the accuracy of this information.

Credits

Authors
Richard Conway
Robin Dewson
Brian Patterson
William A. Sempf

Technical Reviewers
Carl Burnham
Jim Chundevalel
Paul Gorman
Christian Holm
John Maletis
Scott Robertson
David Schultz

Technical Editors
James Hart
Benjamin Hickman
Daniel Maharry
Christian Peak

Commissioning Editor
Andrew Polshaw

Managing Editor
Jan Kolasinski

Project Manager
Beckie Stones

Production & Layout
Neil Lote

Index
Michael Brinkman
Andrew Criddle

Proof Reader
Chris Smith

Cover
Natalie O'Donnell

About the Authors

Richard Conway

Richard Conway started programming BASIC with ZX81 at an early age later graduating to using BASIC and 6502 assembly language, COMAL and Pascal for the BBC B and Archimedes RISC machines. He is an independent software consultant who lives and works in London. He has been using Microsoft technologies for many years and has architected and built enterprise systems for the likes of IBM, Merrill Lynch, and Reuters. He has focused his development on Windows DNA including various tools and languages such as COM+, VB, XML, C++, J++, Biztalk, and more recently, Data Warehousing. He has been actively involved in EAP trials with Microsoft for .NET My Services and the .NET Compact Framework. He has spent the last two years since the release of the technical preview of VS.NET programming proof-of-concept and enterprise system projects in C#. His special area of interest of is Network Security and Cryptography. Richard is a contributor to *C# Today* and *ASP Today*. He is currently finishing a Masters degree in Computing at the OU. Richard can be contacted at techierebel@yahoo.co.uk.

I would like to thank my beautiful wife Suzanne for her never-ending patience and understanding for all the late nights and missed weekends.

Robin Dewson

Robin started out on a Sinclair ZX80 after seeing a demonstration of robots being controlled through a Commodore Pet at Glasgow University. After realizing that 1k memory was not enough to run a power station he soon moved up to larger computing power at the Scottish College of Textiles through an IBM mainframe. After many memorable student days and moving through several more IBM mainframes he saw the light and moved in to personal computers and FoxBASE, FoxPro, VFP through to Visual Basic and SQL Server. After participating in recent beta programs for .NET and SQL Server 2000 he is looking forward to having some spare time to play his two pinball machines.

First of all thanks to Steve Wicks for the sounding board when talking through ideas for this book, Charlie and Debbie Roberts for the best arcade in Norfolk and keeping me sane (!), Cilmara and Jan who I class as my best of friends, everyone at Wrox especially Andrew and Beckie for giving me the chance to write in this book, Jack Mason at Lehman Brothers for the past 3+ years, and Eric Hawk in New York for all those calls during the night. Phill Jupitus and Phil Wilding for the excellent music on 6Music at the BBC www.bbc.co.uk/6music, and Andy Netherway at PinballMania for all his help with my two pinball machines. Of course my family, Julie, Scott, Cameron, and Ellen (yes, Ellen, this does mean you can now play on the pinball machines), and especially my mum and dad who put me on this road in life. Thanks.

Up the Blues!

Brian Patterson

Brian Patterson currently works for Affina, Inc. as a Software Architect. Brian heads up a team of .NET Developers in the construction of CRM Application modules for Affina's Fortune 1000 clients. Brian has been writing for various Visual Basic publications since 1994 and has co-written several .NET-related books, including *Migrating to Visual Basic .NET* and *C# Bible*. Brian is exceptionally well rounded and in his spare time he likes to program, write about programming, and read about programming. You can generally find him posting in the MSDN newgroups or you can reach him by e-mail at BrianDPatterson@msn.com.

William A. Sempf

Bill Sempf is co-author of *Professional Visual Basic .NET* published by Wrox Press. He is an experienced Internet strategist with a ten-year track record of using technology to help organizations accomplish specific business objectives. A Microsoft Certified Professional, Certified Internet Business Strategist, and member of the International Webmaster's Association, Bill has built nearly one hundred dynamic web sites for startups and Fortune 50 companies alike.

Currently, Bill is a Senior Consultant at Paros Business Partners, and owner of Products Of Innovative New Technology. He has written several articles on COM, COM+, and .NET technologies for *TechRepublic*, *Internet.com*, and *Inside Web Development journal*. Web Services are rapidly becoming a passion of Bill's and he is quite certain they are going to be the Next Big Thing. Bill can be reached at bill@sempf.net.

Thanks to Wrox for keeping these quality books on the shelf, and keeping these quality authors in work. Thanks to all my friends, family and fellow programmers for their support.

To my wife Gabrielle for helping with four projects and a book going on all at once: your love, support, and strength go a long way toward keeping me sane. Thank you.

VB.NET

Windows Services

Handbook

Table of Contents

Table of Contents

VB.NET

Windows Services

Handbook

Introduction

Introduction

Windows Services are applications that run in the background and usually have no user interface. In the past, these have usually been created in C++, as Visual Basic did not have the ability to create solid, scalable service applications. With .NET, this has changed. We may not quite have access to all functionality available to C++ programmers, but the .NET Framework has exposed a namespace and a collection of classes to permit the VB programmer to create managed code that runs as a service. This service can be added to the Service Control Manager and viewed and configured using the usual Windows administrative tools.

Windows Services can be used to create server applications that either respond to certain events, or perform some task intermittently. You could create a web server, e-mail server, logging server, messaging server, and more. After reading this book, you will be able to create fully functional server applications that need no intervention from a user. You'll see how to make these services controllable and configurable, scalable and networkable.

Who Is This Book For?

This book is for professional Visual Basic .NET developers who need to create a Windows Service to solve a particular business problem. It takes a ground-up view of Windows Service programming, and assumes no prior experience of service programming either within or outside the .NET environment.

The book assumes throughout that you are already familiar with the Visual Basic .NET language and have experience in using the .NET Framework, creating and compiling projects, and working with the development environment.

What Do You Need to Use This Book?

Windows Service projects cannot be created with Visual Basic .NET Standard Edition, although you can open and compile such projects created in other versions of Visual Studio .NET. A blank Windows Service project is included in the code download file for the book. However, we recommend you use at least Visual Studio .NET Professional to run the code in this book, because it provides better debugging and development tool support, and you may not be able to create all of the samples using just VB.NET Standard Edition.

What Does This Book Cover?

The book covers every stage in developing, debugging, deploying, and scaling Windows Service applications. Here's what you can expect to find in each chapter.

Chapter 1: Introducing Windows Services

This chapter provides an introduction to your first service, detailing some history and how it is now possible to build services in Visual Basic .NET. The main differences between services and standard VB applications are detailed so you know what to expect in service development. In this chapter you are walked through the creation of a simple service, mostly using the wizards available in Visual Studio .NET. By the end of this chapter you will understand exactly what a service is, and what it's for.

Chapter 2: Designing Windows Services

All services fit into certain design models, and knowing what these models are helps in implementing them well. In Visual Basic .NET, only a selection of these models can be adhered to, as VB.NET cannot interact directly with low-level services, such as devices. In this chapter you'll learn what models are available to the VB.NET developer, their advantages and disadvantages, and how to choose between them for a particular task.

Chapter 3: Coding Windows Services

In this chapter, we focus on the finer details of how code executing within a Windows Service can interact with its environment. We'll see how their security context affects what they can and can't do, how services can communicate and log their activities, how they are installed, and how we can debug them.

Chapter 4: Configuring and Controlling Windows Services

This chapter looks at how we can affect Windows Services from the outside, how we can configure them, and how we can control them once they're running. We'll look at the role of the Service Control Manager, and how it can be accessed programmatically, and we'll see how we can use it to pass custom commands to services. We'll also see how we can build interfaces to control a running Windows Service, through a system tray icon, the Web, an MMC snap-in, and through the Windows Management Interface (WMI).

Chapter 5: Network-Oriented Services

A common requirement with Windows Services is to support some sort of networking functionality; indeed, a Windows Service is often the best way to expose a network server on a computer. This chapter discusses some of the issues in deploying Windows Services to remote networked computers, and looks at how we can code network-accessible services.

Chapter 6: Scalability and Performance Issues

Windows Services are often required to provide services for a number of clients at a time, have long uptimes, and perform their activities in the background with minimum intrusion on foreground tasks. This chapter looks at how we can manage memory and threads to create services that are scalable and perform well under loads and for sustained periods.

Chapter 7: Deploying Windows Services

Getting a finished service onto the computer where it will run, and configuring the system so that the service has all the necessary permissions and information it needs to run, is one often-overlooked aspect of service creation. This chapter examines the issues we encounter in putting a service onto a live system, and the automation of deployment through installation scripts.

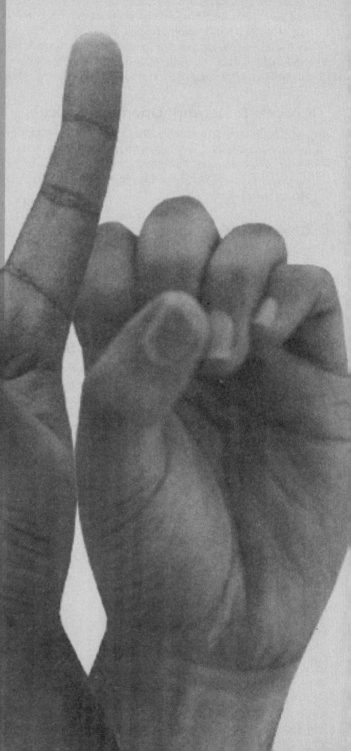

VB.NET

Windows Services

Handbook

1

1

Introducing Windows Services

Windows Services are the next generation of NT Services (as found in Windows 2000 and Windows NT); background tasks that are often loaded by the kernel at startup, independent of any user logging in, and whose lifetime is controlled by the Service Control Manager (SCM), more of which you will learn about later. Find your way to your Services admin tool right now and have a look at the services already started in your own operating system. You should see quite a few.

Services under the Windows operating system have three general defining characteristics:

- ❑ They lack a user interface
- ❑ They have the capability to run under a security context other than the logged on user
- ❑ They have the option of launching without user interaction

Writing a service in VB was complex enough to make learning C++, and writing the service in that instead, seem to be an easier option. This book is important because of this. Thanks to the .NET Framework, creating a Windows Service in VB.NET is now just as easy as it is in C# or C++.

This introductory chapter is going to cover the following topics:

- ❑ A brief history of services
- ❑ How to build a simple Windows Service
- ❑ The `System.ServiceProcess` namespace, which makes VB.NET service programming possible

As you've programmed with VB before, by the end of the chapter, you should have a good appreciation of just how much easier it is to build a rudimentary service. If you're new to service programming, then you'll wonder what all the fuss about. If that is the case, then that will mean the designers of the .NET Framework did their job very well.

A Brief History of Services

This isn't a history book, but having a good idea of where services have come from will give you a good idea of where they are going. Services as a concept have been a mainstay of computing for many years across many operating systems, and the function they serve won't suddenly become redundant with the advent of .NET. Quite the opposite in fact: thanks to their greater usability and the fact they're easier to create, they're likely to be used more often in everyday Enterprise applications.

The UNIX Connection

Many of the event- and time-driven services that Windows uses today are based on processes originally written for UNIX. On that platform, these processes were known as daemons and cron jobs respectively.

Daemons

A daemon isn't a demon. There is nothing satanic about UNIX, despite what many will tell you. The Old English term daemon means 'deified person' and was originally used to describe the angles of a person's personality, much like the proverbial angel and devil that appear on peoples' shoulders when they've a tough decision to make in bad television commercials. The idea behind the UNIX daemons was that they would lurk around in the background until they fired up to help an application do something.

Thus, daemons sit and wait for things: in fact, they still do on UNIX and UNIX-like platforms today. Web servers like Apache, FTP clients, and mail transport agents are examples of daemons. They act on information that arrives – through a network port, or in a directory, or through a user interface.

Later on, as daemons were translated to run under versions of DOS, these new derivatives became know as **terminate and stay resident** (TSR) applications, another term that is still in use today.

Cron

On the other side of services in Unix, there is cron. Its purpose is to start and finish activities based on time (cron – chronological). Server administrators edit the crontab file which contains the list of things to do and when to do them, and cron keeps tabs on the file waiting for the next point for it to spring into action. Meantime, it stays resident in memory, residing in the background.

Both daemons and cron are examples of types of services we can implement using Windows Services, and should give an idea of what has been used in the past. As the NT world snuck into businesses the need was felt for similar functionality, so first, the Windows Scheduler was added to the system.

Scheduler and the Task Manager

Jumping past DOS and TSR applications, which we've mentioned already, early versions of Windows used services (as they were then) to perform event-driven activities and the Windows Scheduler to keep track of time-based jobs. Like cron, it also stayed resident in memory keeping track of time, but rather than a file, kept the jobs it had to start or end in the scheduler registry database, which an administrator could alter using the AT command.

Early Windows also saw the introduction of the SysTray, a service-like program that provided interface-based (forms- and Windows-based) programs the opportunity to run like a service. Still in Windows today (usually in the bottom right of your screen containing a clock and other icons), it still gives applications with a user interface the same opportunity and gives users the opportunity to access services like sound control, networking, and virus scanning.

Although it worked well, Microsoft replaced the scheduler with the Task Manager – a SysTray application – in the IE 4.01 update in 1997. Though those items seem only somewhat related, the Task Manager proved much more stable than the scheduler and is still part of Windows today.

NT Services

The last links between today's Windows services and those we've mentioned so far are known as NT services (they first appeared with the advent of Windows NT). They are closest in design to today's services and in principle are the same. That is, they don't have user interfaces, run in the context of a designated user, and stay resident in memory when not doing anything.

Traditionally, NT Services were closely linked to the operating system or the server's hardware, typically performing one of the following tasks:

- Hardware monitors and drivers
- DCOM Components
- Communication services
- Database management services
- Internet Protocol managers

The tendency for a service to work at a low-level meant that it needed ready access to the many Windows APIs to do its work. Thus, they were usually written in C, C++, or Delphi, which afforded that ready access to the developer.

Visual Basic on the other hand was designed to write form applications and simply not considered by its designers for low-level API calling. Increasingly, as experienced programmers gained in number and the tasks increased in complexity, the advanced functions of VB were exploited. However, these features were often not well tested, and even poorly implemented within the language itself. Those ready armed with a spare development machine and a copy of Dan Appleman's Windows API bible for VB programmers would soon realize exactly how many things they weren't supposed to be able to do – encryption, drawing, and creating services were just three of them.

Fortunately, that imbalance between C++ and VB programmers has been put to rights. With the Common Language Runtime in .NET, VB programmers code against exactly the same API as C# programmers. That means power. VB has been shown to be easier to learn and quicker to code against many times. Now it has the same functionality as the C type languages.

MyFirstService

What better way to start than by building a rudimentary service straight away. We'll generate and install the executable for a service that will write the time to the event log. This admittedly isn't very useful, but it shows many of the essential parts of the service, including the start and stop methods, the logic, and the installer. It will also show the basic steps needed to build and install a service – write the code, write and run the installer, and then start and use (or consume) the service.

1. Open Visual Studio .NET, and click the New Project button on the start page.

2. In the New Project dialog, create a new Visual Basic Windows Service project

3. Change the name to MyFirstService.

4. Make sure your Location is on a local drive, or you'll get security violation errors when debugging.

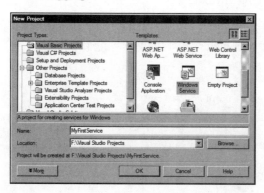

5. Press OK. Visual Studio .NET will create a new project containing the appropriate files and present us with a designer screen, shown below.

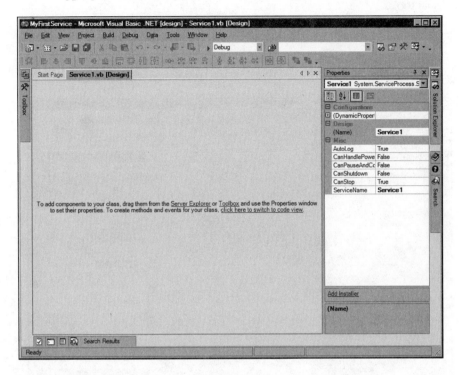

Using the Designer or Coding it Alone

At this point, we have the option of developing our service either visually or by writing all the code ourselves. This may come as something of a surprise, given that services by default have no visual element. You design forms-based applications visually, but you wouldn't think that you design services in this way.

It's actually not as nonsensical as you might think when you consider how Visual Studio .NET was designed to work.

The Designer

Visual Studio .NET is a Rapid Application Development tool, and it acts like one. The Toolbox contains many non-visual components that we can add to the logic at the core of our service as well as WinForms controls that we'd use to build the UI for a forms-base application. Like the controls, all we need do is drag the components we need from the Toolbox onto the designer and the code will be automatically generated.

Of course, we can also the code ourselves – but it would be exactly the same code generated when we use the visual designers. It is your choice, but here we'll start with the visual tools.

6. Go to the Toolbox, and switch to the Components section.

7. Drag an EventLog object and a Timer object from the Toolbox onto the designer area.

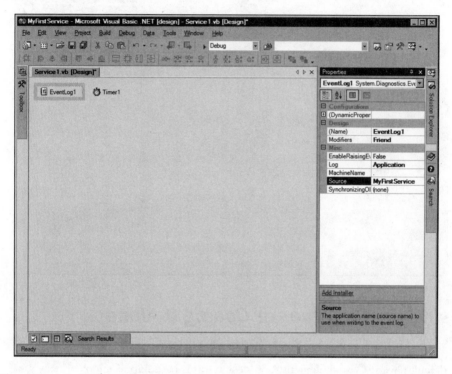

Like a Timer in VB6, we have a visual representation of each non-visual element, and, more importantly, a property panel to match as well. The code to create and initialize each component has also been generated. This visual RAD approach should not be dismissed just because it hasn't been used before in creating services. It's a quick and reliable way to generate the startup code before you have to get your hands dirty.

8. Select the EventLog object on the designer and change the Log property in the Properties panel to Application.

9. Still with the EventLog object, change its Source property to MyFirstService.

We'll look for these names later on in the Event Viewer as we search for evidence the service is running.

Code View

Let's see the code that VS .NET has auto-generated for us.

10. Right-click on the Designer window and select View Code from the context menu that appears.

As you can see, VS.NET has generated a fair amount of boilerplate code that you would have had to write yourself if you chose to code the service alone, so using the designer has turned out to be a good idea. Of particular interest, if you expand the Component Designer generated code section, you will find the code to set up the EventLog and Timer entry in the InitializeComponent() method.

```
Friend WithEvents EventLog1 As System.Diagnostics.EventLog
Friend WithEvents Timer1 As System.Timers.Timer
<System.Diagnostics.DebuggerStepThrough()>
  Private Sub InitializeComponent()

  Me.EventLog1 = New System.Diagnostics.EventLog()
  Me.Timer1 = New System.Timers.Timer()
  CType(Me.EventLog1,
    System.ComponentModel.ISupportInitialize).BeginInit()
  CType(Me.Timer1,
    System.ComponentModel.ISupportInitialize).BeginInit()


  '
  'EventLog1
  '
  Me.EventLog1.Log = "Application"
  Me.EventLog1.Source = "MyFirstService"


  '
  'Timer1
  '
  Me.Timer1.Enabled = True


  '
  'Service1
  '
  Me.ServiceName = "Service1"
  CType(Me.EventLog1,
    System.ComponentModel.ISupportInitialize).EndInit()
  CType(Me.Timer1, System.ComponentModel.ISupportInitialize).EndInit()

End Sub
```

Take heed of the warning directly above InitializeComponent() and leave this piece of code to VS.NET. We have the rest of the file to add our own code to, and it will need guidance if we're to make the service do something useful.

Adding Some Functionality

Remember that the goal of our first service here is to write the time to the event log after a given period has elapsed. We'll set the timer to run as soon as the service is started and end when the service is stopped. In between these two events, the only action the service need take is to write to the event log when the given time has elapsed. This we can do by writing a `Timer.Elapsed` event handler.

Services nearly always require some sort of initialization when started and cleanup when stopped so VS.NET auto-generates blank handlers for both of these events by default. We'll fill in both of them.

11. Add the following code to the `OnStart` method to enable the timer:

```
Protected Overrides Sub OnStart(ByVal args() As String)
    'Set timer interval to 6 seconds
    Timer1.Interval = 6000

    'Enable the timer. This will throw the Elapsed event every Interval
    Timer1.Enabled = True
End Sub
```

12. Before you add code to a service's `OnStop()` handler, ask yourself the simple questions. "How do I undo everything I did in the `OnStart()` method? What will clean up the service completely?" When you've the answer, that's what you add to the `OnStop()` method. In the case of this service, the answer is very simple.

```
Protected Overrides Sub OnStop()
    'Disable the timer
    Timer1.Enabled = False
End Sub
```

13. Last but not least, add the following code for the `Timer1.Elapsed` event handler that writes the time to the event log.

```
Private Sub Timer1_Elapsed(ByVal sender As System.Object, _
    ByVal e As System.Timers.ElapsedEventArgs) Handles Timer1.Elapsed

    'Write the time to the event log.
    EventLog1.WriteEntry(DateTime.Now.ToShortTimeString().ToString())

End Sub
```

That's all the code we need for the purposes of this demonstration. All we need do now is compile and run the code.

14. Build the solution and check for errors. (*Ctrl + Shift + B*)

15. Click Debug / Start. (*F5*)

Unfortunately, that's not all there is to it, as the error message that appears soon after pressing *F5* tells us.

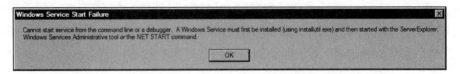

Windows Service Start Failure

Cannot start service from the command line or a debugger. A Windows Service must first be installed (using installutil.exe) and then started with the ServerExplorer, Windows Services Administrative tool or the NET START command.

OK

Creating an Installer for the Service

It turns out that services can't be run from the Visual Studio environment by pressing *F5*, because they require the Service Control Manager to function properly, and in order for the SCM to run the service, it must have certain meta-information about it and the resources it requires.

Fortunately, Visual Studio .NET not only includes references to pre-built classes that provide installation tools, but also wizards to ease the configuration of these classes. Building an installer for the service is easier than building the service itself.

1. Switch to the designer window for Service1.vb and click on the designer window so that neither of the components is selected.

2. Press *F4* to view the Properties panel. It should be displaying the properties for the service, as shown below.

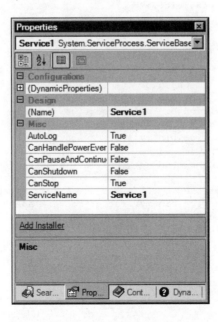

3. Click the Add Installer link at the bottom of the properties window. VS.NET will add a new class called `ProjectInstaller` to our project and pre-set it up with two components, a `ServiceProcessInstaller` and a `ServiceInstaller`.

4. Select the `ServiceProcessInstaller` and change its `Account` property to `LocalSystem`.

At this point, we could add a setup project to the solution that would hold a copy of the compiled service, run the installers associated with it and install it, but that's a bit ambitious at the moment. Instead, we'll use VS .NET's built-in install utility, `InstallUtil.exe`.

5. Rebuild `MyFirstService.exe` (*Ctrl + Shift + B*)

6. Now start up VS.NET's command-prompt window. You'll find this in the Start Menu under All Programs | VS .NET | VS .NET Tools. Use this rather than the standard command-prompt window which won't necessarily be aware of all VS.NET's environment variables.

7. Now navigate to the folder containing our compiled `.exe` file. The default location is My Documents\Visual Studio Projects\MyFirstService\bin.

8. Run the command `installutil MyFirstService.exe`.

`InstallUtil` should install the service without a hitch, keeping us informed of its progress. Here's an abbreviated version of the output you'll see in the command prompt.

```
>installutil MyFirstService.exe
Microsoft (R) .NET Framework Installation utility Version 1.0.3705.0
Copyright (C) Microsoft Corporation 1998-2001. All rights reserved.

Running a transacted installation.

Beginning the Install phase of the installation.
See the contents of the log file for the f:\visual studio
projects\myfirstservice\bin\myfirstservice.exe assembly's progress.
The file is located at f:\visual studio
projects\myfirstservice\bin\myfirstservice.InstallLog.

The Install phase completed successfully, and the Commit phase is
beginning.
See the contents of the log file for the f:\visual studio
projects\myfirstservice\bin\myfirstservice.exe assembly's progress.
The file is located at f:\visual studio
projects\myfirstservice\bin\myfirstservice.InstallLog.

The Commit phase completed successfully.

The transacted install has completed.
```

Recall that in Step 4, we set the `ServiceProcessInstaller's Account` property to `LocalSystem`, indicating that it should run under the Local System account. If we had left it set to `User`, `InstallUtil` would have prompted us for the service login – an account with local administrator access. So then, the security context of a service isn't necessarily that of the user currently logged on. It could be the System account, or a specially created custom account.

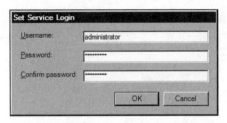

Note that `InstallUtil` is a transacted install procedure by default. If something fails along the way, the whole install routine to that point will be rolled back to the system's original state.

Finding our Service

With our service successfully installed, all we need to do now is find it and start it up. Services are set to Manual by default, so nothing's going to happen in the event log unless we get `MyFirstService` running.

1. Return to Visual Studio .NET and open the Server Explorer. We'll be able to access the SCM straight from here.

2. If the machine you've installed the service onto isn't listed under the Servers node, add it by right-clicking on Servers and selecting Add Server...

We didn't change the name of our service before we installed it, so it should still be called `Service1`.

3. Expand the Services node under your local development machine and find Service1.

4. Right-click on Service1 and select Start.

5. In the Server Explorer, change to the Event Viewer and find the Application log.

6. Under Service1, we can see the log entries that the ServiceProcessInstaller has made on our behalf and under MyFirstService, the service group we created, we can see that the time is being posted as expected.

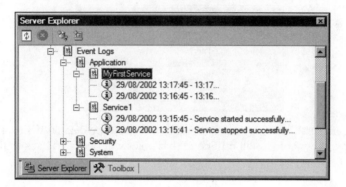

So we now have a fully functional windows service written with a tiny amount of VB.NET code in about ten minutes. To clean up this demo, we need to stop the service and then uninstall it.

1. Still in the Server Explorer, navigate to Service1 again under the Services node. Right click it and select Stop.

2. Switch back to the VS.NET command-prompt window and run the command `installutil /u MyFirstService.exe` to uninstall the service.

Debugging our Service

Of course, this simple exercise isn't that realistic. How many times have you written an application that needed no debugging whatsoever? Debugging a service with VS.NET is much the same as debugging any other application, but because we can't just run a service by pressing *F5*, likewise we can't just step into a service and start debugging it. We have to approach it indirectly and attach the debugger to the process the service is running in.

The method is still quite straightforward:

1. Compile the service and install it on your system.

2. Start it with the Service Control Manager.

3. In VS.NET, click on Debug | Processes to bring up a list of the currently running processes that we can attach the debugger to. If you can't find the name of your service in the main panel, try checking the Show System Processes box and looking again.

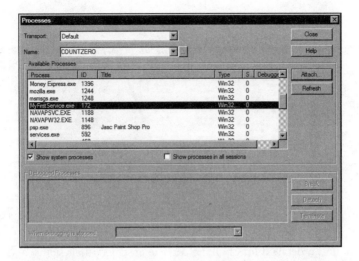

4. Once you've found the service, click Attach....

5. Make sure that Common Language Runtime is checked in the next dialog and press OK.

You'll now be able to debug the service as you would any other application. When you stop the debugger, VS.NET will detach itself from the service process automatically. We'll look at debugging a service more closely in Chapter 3.

The User Experience

Before we start in on the classes in the .NET Framework that make the development of a service such a simple thing, let's have quick look at how users approach services – if at all. So far, we've already seen that services differ in their creation from normal applications in several ways. The same is true in the way users interact with services.

In most cases, users don't actually know services exist even when they're interacting with them. After all, the purpose of a Windows Service is to provide invisible functionality to the user – it doesn't have a UI. In general, user interaction with a service is limited to:

❑ Working with the Service Control Manager

❑ Reading any messages (error messages, status reports, etc.) that the service leaves in the Windows event logs

The closest we'll get to a user interface for a service is the Service Controller snap-in to the Microsoft Management Controller. In Windows 2000 \ Windows XP, you'll find it as part of the Computer Management administrative tool from the Start menu.

Figure 1

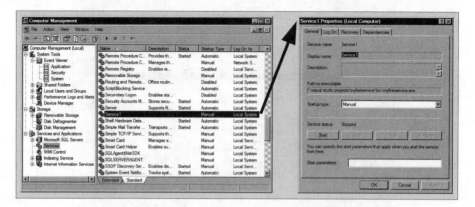

Initially, you'll find a detailed list of all the services installed, their status, and their startup type. Double-click on a service and you'll get a second dialog (shown above) providing you with basic functionality, like start, stop, pause, and the ability to specify as whose account the service should log on.

In contrast to this nearly-write-only arrangement in the SCM, the Event Viewer offers us a read-only interface to our services. As we saw earlier on, it's in the various event logs on the service's local server that we'll find any status or error messages generated by a service. Even if the user is utilizing the service through the network from another server, log entries and service alerts will remain on the service's local server.

The System.ServiceProcess Namespace

We've already established that the .NET Framework was designed so that VB.NET users could do the same as C# users, but the main reason service development is a lot easier is the System.ServiceProcess namespace. This provides the classes, methods, properties, exceptions, and events that allow the creation of Windows Services.

Under this namespace, you'll find ten classes as follows:

- **ServiceBase**
  Is the base class for any .NET-based service class written as part of a service application. ServiceBase must be inherited from and derived when creating a new service class.

- **ServiceController**
  Represents any currently existing Windows service and allows you to connect to, start, stop, and generally manipulate it.

❏ **ServiceControllerPermission**
Allows you to set the level of security and permissions for service controllers trying to access your service.

❏ **ServiceControllerPermissionAttribute**
Used to secure access to the service by associating a `SecurityAction`, for example, to a custom security attribute. Use this class only for declarative security.

❏ **ServiceControllerPermissionEntry**
Defines the smallest unit of code access security permission for a `ServiceController` to the service.

❏ **ServiceControllerPermissionEntryCollection**
Contains a strongly typed collection of `ServiceControllerPermissionEntry` objects each defining different levels of code access to the service for different `ServiceControllers`.

❏ **ServiceInstaller**
Manages the information written to the registry about each of the services within a given executable. Its properties include service-level information like the name of the service or the start type of each service. Methods include rolling back the installation of a given service, or the logging of problems encountered.

❏ **ServiceProcessDescriptionAttribute**
Specifies a description for a property or event. This could be the long description of the service itself or a description of an event noted by the service.

❏ **ServiceProcessInstaller**
Handles the writing of information to the registry for all services in a given executable. The properties we would set in a given instance of the `ServiceProcessInstaller` might include a specific NT Account for the service to utilize, or a simple username and password pair. The `ServiceProcessInstaller` also accepts context information about services already installed.

❏ **TimeoutException**
Defines the exception that is thrown when a specified timeout related in some way to the running of the service has expired.

Several of these classes will only ever be used in advanced scenarios and some we've already used. More obviously, we used both the installer classes in our earlier example. What we may not have noticed, however, is that we also used a third class – `ServiceBase`.

The ServiceBase Class

As the name would suggest, every .NET Windows Service is created using classes derived from the `System.ServiceProcess.ServiceBase` class, which defines the basic methods for the control of a service, as follows.

- ❑ `OnStart()`
- ❑ `OnStop()`
- ❑ `OnPause()`
- ❑ `OnContinue()`
- ❑ `OnShutdown()`

A developer needs to override these methods as appropriate to define the behavior of their own services. In our brief example for instance, we needed only to override the `OnStart()` and `OnStop()` methods. `ServiceBase` also defines a set of properties for the SCM's benefit announcing the capabilities of the new service:

- ❑ `CanHandlePowerEvent`
- ❑ `CanPauseAndContinue`
- ❑ `CanShutdown`
- ❑ `CanStop`

> *The existence of the `ServiceBase` class neatly points out the reason why we primarily use object oriented languages for the creation of services. Since the services must by design use inheritance and polymorphism, C++ has historically been the best language for their production. Because VB.NET now supports all of these OO features, services can now be developed in this language.*

Looking Ahead

So then, in twenty pages we've completed our rough guide to creating Windows Services. There's much more detail to be gone into, but we've covered the general gist of things. The rest of this book will take us through an advanced tour of the Windows Services architecture, including design, programming, configuration, and deployment – among other topics.

In the next chapter, we'll look at when to use Windows Services and when not to. It isn't always obvious in what situations they are the best solutions. We'll focus on the five main types of services, and their real-world counterparts.

- Monitor/listener

- Agent

- Quartermaster/Resource Pooler

- Switch Board

- Business Object

With the theory out of the way, Chapter 3 will build on our work here and create a moderately complex Windows Service, looking closely at the classes available in the `System.ServiceProcess` namespace for us to use. We'll revisit the topic of service debugging as well. This chapter is a blueprint for real-world code and processes.

While Windows Services by definition aren't interactive applications, that doesn't mean users will never need to configure them. The most commonly used method of providing a user interface is via the system tray. In Chapter 4, we'll be looking at when and how to add a user interface to your Windows Service and how to make it effective.

One task services are particularly good at given their tendency to lurk in the background, is polling system networks and facilitating the operation of distributed applications across those networks. Whether it's supplying the quote of the day to users as they log in, or working as a conduit for SOAP messages and proxy-stub remoting set ups, services are always handy. In Chapter 5, we'll look at a series of services that implement classes within the `System.Net` namespace and its various functionality.

Of course, no one's going to be pleased if your service slows to the pace of a tranquilized slug when a few users start using it, especially as it could drag their system to a halt with it. The `ServiceBase` namespace provides functionality closer to the operating system than most of the .NET Framework, and therefore we need a closer look at performance issues. In Chapter 6, we'll look at the problems associated with performance, like threading, memory use, unsafe code, and scalability, and how to go about avoiding them.

Finally, yet importantly, in Chapter 7 we'll be looking at the issues involved in deploying a Windows Service, especially:

- OS versions

- Installing and uninstalling

- Windows services database

- Security

The deployment of a Windows Service using your own installer is significantly more complex than deploying it using `InstallUtil` as we did earlier. It's in this final chapter of the book that we'll get to grips with those particular tricky bits.

Summary

The .NET Framework has brought much to the beleaguered VB programmer – a truly object-oriented version of VB, and equal access to the APIs and classes that C++\C# developers have are the two main ones. It's thanks to these two gifts that VB programmers can now develop Windows Services.

In this first chapter, we've learned quite a few things. In particular:

❑ How UNIX daemons evolved into the Windows services we know today

❑ How to build, compile, install, run, and debug a simple service with Visual Studio .NET

❑ That the `System.ServiceProcess` namespace contains all the classes necessary for developing services and what those classes do.

The rest of the book will give a much more in-depth look at the world of Windows Services.

VB.NET

Windows Services

Handbook

2

2

Designing Windows Services

Now we have a vehicle for Windows Services, how does this fit into what we do every day? Since this is a new ability for VB programmers, we need to look at how it fits into our existing job duties, how to plan for Windows Services in our documentation, how to think about using these services, and when they are useful. We need to design a few examples, and discuss how things might work, because designing for Windows Services isn't like the normal data-access application design most programmers daily do.

In this design-oriented chapter, you won't see much code. However, you will see two primary topics:

- ❑ How to design services
  - The categories Windows Services naturally fall into
  - Whether there are standard services
  - What questions need to be answered before building a service
- ❑ How to design for services
  - How to leverage the services to solve our problems
  - The tools that are available for diagramming Windows Services
  - The design patterns available

Types of Services

Windows services, which are actually all daemons, come in several different flavors. Conceptually, you can build five essential types of services – irrespective of operating system. Certain requirements need to be fulfilled regardless of how you go about creating them. We'll cover each in detail. The different design types are shown below:

- Monitor/listener
- Agent
- Quartermaster
- Switchboard
- Business Object

Beyond these design types, we find seven physical types present in the `System.ServiceProcess.ServiceType` enumeration:

- `Adapter`
- `KernelDriver`
- `InteractiveProcess`
- `FileSystemDriver`
- `RecognizerDriver`
- `Win32OwnProcess`
- `Win32ShareProcess`

The last two of these seven physical types are handled by the Service Control Manager. They are coded by the managed code in the CLR, and we will be blending these to the five Design Patterns to build the services.

Design Patterns

The five conceptual types of services define all of the tasks that a continuously running service would possibly perform. They are all examples of the **State** design pattern as defined in Design Patterns, Gamma, Helm, Johnson, and Vlissides (ISBN: 0-201-63361-2). The State design pattern allows an object to alter its behavior when its internal state changes.

Technically, these objects are internalizing, through polymorphism, some of the properties of another object in the system, such as the clock or a port. Polymorphism is best described as the new VB.NET feature that allows for the overriding and overloading of methods. Therefore, we don't often change the class of a service when the state changes, as defined in the State pattern. Instead, we can simply change the overloaded method called.

> We have to answer the two questions of service design while selecting a pattern, which are "What is the action that triggers the service?" and "What state is maintained by the service?" The answer to these questions will often determine much about the pattern of the service.

These are design patterns, not designs, holding the common trait of maintaining some state for the system. Design patterns are the cookie cutters that we use to make our neat shapes to build software. We use these cookie cutters to generate the designs of the final services we need to run our system.

Monitor/Listener

Sometimes called a Watcher, this design pattern monitors a file or listens at a port, and notifies someone or something or causes an action when an event occurs. FTP Servers, SMTP Servers, and Web Servers are excellent examples of Listeners. Log analyzers and triggers are examples of Monitors.

As to the answers to the questions, we find that they have a similar direction. The act of listening is the state that is maintained, and hearing what is listened to is the trigger.

Agent

Unix Cron and atd are agents – services that use time to perform tasks in the background. The best example of this is the Microsoft Message Queuing system MSMQ – though there is a long list, since tools like the Windows Task Schedulers are technically agents too – it watches the clock instead of a file or port, and handles tasks in the background.

Essentially the agent takes an action on behalf of the system, user, or (probably absent) Administrator, and gets out of the way. The state that is maintained in the Agent design pattern is the awareness of events or time. The trigger is the time set by the administrator between the events.

Quartermaster

The Quartermaster allocates very scarce resources efficiently, and improves performance. In the standard Windows XP installation, the Protected Storage service is an example of a quartermaster. It provides access to the resource pool of cryptographic keys and similar information in such a way that the security is not compromised and data integrity is not an issue. A Quartermaster provides pre-initialized resources to the requesting client. In a conceptual sense, you could think of a database connection pool, or a thread pool, as a Quartermaster too.

Rarely does one *have to* use a Quartermaster design pattern. It is a performance enhancement technique, and not a solution to a specific design problem. It is a necessary pattern for certain problems, however. The state that is maintained is the status of the resources. The trigger is the request of a resource – the quartermaster is asked to serve by one of its registered clients.

Switchboard

A switchboard is a service that intercepts a generic request and directs it to a handler – usually another service. For instance, the NT Wolfpack, the original server farm software for Windows, is a Switchboard service, accepting a call to a central machine and distributing the request to the next machine in line to handle requests.

As with a real telephone switchboard, we can think of this design pattern as a hub that connects clients to a service that is less busy or more apt to be able to service the request, thus making the actual address of the necessary resource irrelevant to the client. The state that is maintained in this service is the status of the resources, like a Quartermaster, and the trigger is similar too – that of a request from a registered client. The major difference is that the resource or service the client is directed to isn't wholly managed by the switchboard. Again, this is similar to a real telephone switchboard; it knows when a line is busy, and how many calls are waiting on it, but doesn't actually manage the time or other resources of the person at the other end.

Business Object

Sometimes, we need our business objects to manage state, in case they are needed by an application. This is sort of a catchall category, because all of the resources discussed up until now have been business objects, but they had specific patterns of design. If something we are building doesn't have a specific pattern, it is a generic business object.

State maintained is usually the value of properties. The State Server for IIS is a good example of this, with actual `Session` and `Application` objects available for property storage. The trigger is the request of an application.

Windows Types

A necessary set of services is only developed in Assembler or C++ as unmanaged code. These include those services closest to the operating system, like the device drivers and file managers noted below, and are rarely managed by a controller like the `ServiceController`. These are the applications that are often started at the BIOS level, and that show up in our task manager even though they are not Windows Services, and were never consciously loaded.

Most importantly, we do not cover these services in this book. We can interact with them under some circumstances, and we know their type by interrogating their `ServiceType` enumeration with the `ServiceController` object.

Adapter

The Adapter type represents a hardware device that requires its own driver. Those files (usually Dynamic Link Libraries) managed by the operating system that deal with hardware directly fall into this ServiceType.

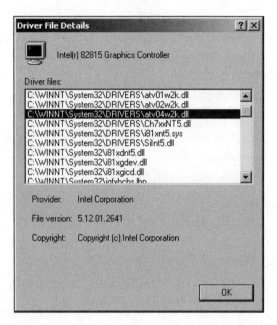

KernelDriver

Working alongside the FileSystemDriver (mentioned shortly), this type of service manages low-level hardware devices, like hard drives, processors, and motherboards. These low-level items of code will never be seen unless writing hardware drivers.

InteractiveProcess

An InteractiveProcess communicates with the desktop, and therefore the user. These are services with user interfaces, often residing in the SysTray. Antiviral software uses the InteractiveProcess model a lot, both speaking with the system at the boot level and at the user level.

Now, let it be known that we can write services with user interfaces in VB.NET, but they are not InteractiveProcesses. Our services will always be a Win32SharedProcess, and won't have the kinds of access to the hardware found in this low-level service. For instance, our service couldn't directly access the UART, and allow the user to manipulate codes coming directly from a modem.

FileSystemDriver

As one would imagine, this is a driver for the file system (FAT32, NTFS). This is deep code, and not something that we usually can see with the operating system. FileSystemDrivers work at the kernel level, and interact with the KernelDriver types.

The FileSystemDriver concept lives in the UNIX space too. The Linux file system is managed by modules similar to the FileSystemDriver Windows type.

RecognizerDriver

This is a bootstrap service used to determine the types of file systems present on the system at startup. It interacts with the FileSystemDriver to load the file system, like FAT32 or NTFS.

.NET Types

Two types of managed services can be created with .NET. Because of the Common Language Runtime, these are language independent but, of course, this book will focus on implementing them in Visual Basic .NET.

Win32OwnProcess

This Win32 executable can be started by the Service Control Manager (or SCM, sometimes called SCuM); it obeys its own protocol, and runs in its own process. This service must implement all of the methods understood by the Service Controller, specifically OnStart() and OnStop(). Standalone services, like the Fax service, are often Win32OwnProcess types. These types may use information from other devices, but they are rarely used by other services.

Win32ShareProcess

A Win32ShareProcess is like a Win32OwnProcess, but it shares processes with other Win32 services. Services that are often shown as dependencies to other services, like the Telephony, Print Spooler, RPC Handler, and Plug-and-Play services for the Fax Service, are Win32ShareProcess types. If you are writing a service that will be used by other services, you are writing a Win32ShareProcess.

How These Interact

Interaction of services is what matters. Microsoft has built a careful web of services that heighten the scalability and stability of the Windows system. Most of the time, we won't be rebuilding the Windows operating system from scratch, but rather will be interacting with existing services. Why build something when Windows does it for you? The important part is in understanding how the design patterns and service types work together to make software most compatible with what is happening under the hood.

Throughout the rest of the chapter, you will see how the design patterns interact with existing services, as well as seeing new Windows Services that can be built. We'll also examine issues like what we can do, how to draw it, and how to think about it.

What Services Can Do

Now that we have the option of writing Windows Services using VB.NET, what can we do with them? Essentially, any time we need to have a piece of our code running all the time, waiting, watching, or prepared to accept an event, we can use a Windows Service.

Management of Systems

Be careful whom you talk to about this. Too much discussion of the power of Windows Services around the system administrators in your department can lead to a significant increase in programming projects. Of course, you could always look at it as job security.

Windows Services is how Microsoft chooses to have its systems administered. Nearly everything of interest to a power user is available in the Service Control Manager. Thanks to the .NET Framework, custom applications used for management can also be hosted by the SCM, providing a One-Stop Shop for the management of NT Systems.

The most common example of a type of management application that can be made into a Windows Service is a .VBS script that is run in the Scheduler. I'm sure we can all think of tasks we have running that way, but here are a few examples:

❑ Movement of files on a schedule; for instance, the distribution of image files that are sent by FTP to a central server

❑ Watching for service failures on important servers

❑ Confirmation of events

❑ Notification of occurrences

❑ A combination of the above; much more difficult to do with off-the-shelf software

Custom Integration between an Application and Server

On the application development side, Windows Services provide a fantastic conduit for tasks we need a server to do. If you were building a client/server application, the server side of things could be well managed with a Windows Service, especially if you were not using a standard service like DCOM or IIS as the entry point to the server.

Windows Services are excellent for building complex interactions in sophisticated large systems. Designing these systems is a massive task, and it exceeds the scope of a chapter like this, so describing these interactions will not make too much sense here.

Providing Services to Clients and Devices

This seems similar to custom application integration, but it isn't. Imagine the above example as internal piping, and this example as external piping.

For instance, the ActiveSync software (used for synchronizing data between a PocketPC device and a PC) is a client service – it doesn't run in the SCM, but the same design concepts apply. Most antiviral programs have onboard HTTP, POP3, or MAPI ports to support checking inbound traffic for viruses before passing it on to the actual client. These applications are using services as interaction with the outside.

Often, client services like these use the Agent design pattern, and sometimes they are implemented as SysTray applications and placed in the Startup folder of Windows. Now, with the ease of developing Windows Services, we can place them in the SCM and have greater control and less visibility.

Security

Security is a primary concern of all application developers – or at least it should be. Windows Services can circumspectly or openly watch files and ports, users and network activity.

Intrusion detection systems often make use of Windows Services that are close to the hardware, providing an unprecedented look at the network packets flowing through a system. We can't get that kind of access through the framework, but we can get close.

Some of the ways Windows Services can help us with security include:

❑ Watching FTP, IIS, and custom port activity

❑ Watching files for unexpected activity, such as editing

❑ Timed alteration of file circumstances (location, state) to defeat intrusion

❑ Application-centric activity logging, to log user, file, and port activity in one place, for instance

What We Need to Know

A number of questions need to be answered before we can start developing these services. Kevin Miller in Wrox's *Professional NT Services* (ISBN: 1-86100-130-4) provides a great overview to these issues, and they have changed little since. Let's look at today's version of that list of questions.

The Usage Pattern Used

The activity trigger will help you determine what usage pattern you are looking at. A *Monitor* is notified if something has happened to a particular resource. Sometimes this can simply be that the resource has existed for a particular amount of time, or perhaps that a file has been written to. *Agents* also often use time schedules, or work from a client request. They provide an asynchronous path to completion of some activity.

Quartermasters often monitor the statistics of scarce resources, and provide them as needed. In addition, they respond to requests from clients for these resources then clean up afterward, in the background. *Business Objects* are just as they sound, and react to client requests. They are often replaced by COM+, as we'll see below. Finally, *Switchboards* respond to a client request for a connection and make the connection in the background.

There is no switch in Visual Studio .NET that says: "This is an Agent service". The usage pattern is a guideline – the first step in the design process, as it were. It gives us a level to check the accuracy of our design decisions. When we have to determine the best way to solve a problem, we can return to the usage and ask, "Does this meet the needs of the usage pattern?"

What are the Security Considerations?

We need to consider the security of the service itself. We have a number of questions to answer about the environment in which our service runs, despite its design pattern.

- ❑ Whom should the service impersonate?
- ❑ Does it need access to a unique or secure resource?
- ❑ What will the service do to protect itself?
- ❑ Should it leave an audit trail?
- ❑ Does it require data encryption?

Let's look at some of these specifically.

Account

The service has the choice of running under a user account, the Administrator account, and the System account. There is also an option to create a service that runs in the context of the local user, but that isn't the default option, nor is it recommended for most uses. User access changes and people change companies and departments.

We have four actual settings for the `Account` property of the `ServiceProcess` object:

❑   **User** represents a single valid user on the network, and this is entered at install time.

❑   **LocalService** is a special account that represents extensive local privileges.

❑   **LocalSystem** is the System account that is non-priviledged on the system, and anonymous on the network.

❑   **NetworkService** isn't privileged on the system, but it gives the computer's credentials on the network.

User Impersonation

There are times when the service might need to impersonate the logged in user in order to gain access to certain resources.

Protection

Two topics raise their head when dealing with how the service protects its own data. First we need to protect stored data; the second problem concerns transmission of network information.

Stored information can be saved by 'most any account the service is set to, then the ACL for that file can be adjusted to protect the information. Keep in mind that this kind of storage is most often compromised by crackers, so perhaps even encryption is necessary for very sensitive information.

Data transmission is another security issue that can probably be solved by encryption.

How Control Requests are handled

As discussed in Chapter 1, a number of required or highly recommended events should be supported by all services. One of the design decisions we need to face is how we will handle all of those requests. The events in question are handled by the `OnStart()`, `OnPause()`, `OnContinue()`, and `OnStop()` methods.

Only `OnStart()` and `OnStop()` are required. The primary thing to remember is not to tie up a required resource for the lifetime of the service – which is easier to do than you might first think. Stopping the service suggests that the service finish its existing iteration or activity, and no longer accepts any new requests during that time.

Pause and continue have some interesting problems. For instance, does a paused object accept requests and queue them? Is state maintained through a pause? On continue, are all queued requests run at once, or are they spaced out? What about the Monitor and its timing loop; does pause wait for the completion of the loop? These very specific questions are examples of the depth to which design should go before coding begins.

Remember, we cannot answer these questions here. They are very closely connected to the design of the service, and there is no generic answer.

The Administration Details

All .NET Windows Services written in managed code use the SCM for administration, but you need to consider more. Most importantly, you need to decide who can administer the service. By default, only administrators can manage services, but if others need to manage the service, arrangements must be made. In addition, you must decide what will be available for administration.

Whether the Service Will Leave Logs

There are two likely log types for a service. First, you can leave the evidence of events – especially start and stop – in the Event Log. After all, it is called the *event* log. In addition, you can save performance data in the performance monitor – another adequately named service. This is remarkably easy to do, as you saw in Chapter 1. The logs have object interfaces now that are available to VB.NET programmers, and creating access from a service to one of these logs is now nearly trivial and recommended.

When Not to Write a Service

Times when not to write a service include:

- ❑ When one is available already – don't write an HTTP handler unless there is a very good reason. IIS does a good job already.

- ❑ When trying to pass or queue messages – BizTalk handles message passing well, and MSMQ does an excellent job of queuing. MSMQ has the added benefit of being freely available for your use.

❏   When you can use COM+ – Business Objects may not need to be an always-on service, sometimes Just-in-Time activation will be good enough. COM+ provides that service with the `System.EnterpriseServices` namespace. Of course, when maintaining state, a Business Object design pattern might be necessary.

With .NET, it might be easier to build than buy, which is why the purchase decision isn't above. Nonetheless, sometimes you can spend less money by discovering a piece of software out there that does exactly what you need.

Diagramming

In this section, you will see some examples of diagrams that can be used to represent Windows Services. You should find many of these useful in describing the processes involved.

How to Describe Windows Services

Windows Services often show up in state diagrams as things that machines do that they don't normally do. As said previously, if in a design meeting, a developer is asked, "How is that going to happen?" that is often a case to build a Windows Service. Sometimes it is purchased; sometimes an object is put in MSMQ or COM+. With the .NET Framework, however, we can make some different decisions.

Look at the following example architecture:

Figure 1

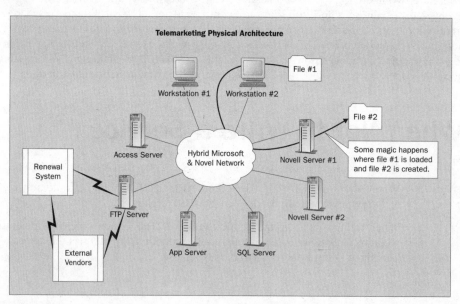

How is the above system going to know when to move the files? There is no good way in Visual Basic COM development. With the Monitor design pattern, however, we have the opportunity to keep an eye on files.

So how would we diagram that? We just did. There is no standardized way to show service type ability – it is more or less assumed in a static architecture diagram like the one above. A class diagram has the same problem. It just shows that the logic within the service is utilized at some point during the execution of the application.

A diagram does exist that shows action over time and it demonstrates the need for something like a Windows service nicely. It is the UML diagram called the Collaboration, or Transition, diagram, shown below in Figure 2:

Figure 2

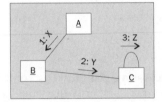

UML and Services

The transition diagram is used to show changes in a system over time. Since Windows Services are all about changes, and time, it would seem to be a match – and it is. The fact is, though, that there isn't a sign that says "Hey, put a Windows Service here!" The biggest clue to the developer is that feeling that Windows just won't do something that needs to be done.

Figure 3

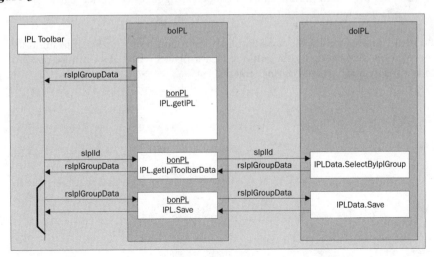

In this diagram, we are in a position to give a registry key from a time card system to a user when they log in as part of the `bonIPL.IPL.getIPL()` method. If there is no obvious Windows API for this device, we're stuck. Though we could just have our application call to the remote system as needed, there is a good chance we could overwhelm it.

Therefore, this is a good use for a Quartermaster service – which is exactly what happened in this system. We had to write it in C++ because it was before the CLR (back in 1999) but a Windows Service solved the problem the only way we knew how.

In the design process – that's exactly what it comes down to. If it is a state/trigger issue, and it isn't obvious how to solve the problem, then it is a job for a Windows Service. Use architecture diagrams and UML, especially transactional diagrams, to decide when you need to use one.

Summary

The design of Windows Services is a significant topic, probably deserving of several chapters. We managed to answer a number of questions in a short period, including the following:

❑   Understanding how the Conceptual and Physical types of services interact.

❑   Learning that UML and Process Flow could effectively show the design of Windows Services

❑   Determining there are number of tasks that can make use of the key features of Windows Services

❑   Asking the important questions: "What triggers the service?" and "What state is maintained?"

In the next chapter, we'll look at coding and controlling services. Keep in mind these design patterns discussed, and begin looking for places where they can be used to solve business problems on current projects.

VB.NET

Windows Services

Handbook

3

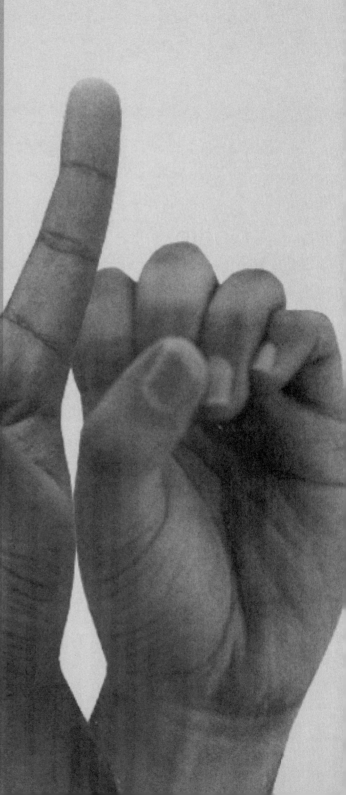

3

Coding Windows Services

We now have a good overview of how to build Windows Services, and of the various roles they can be given within an operating system. From this point on, we'll be getting into the practical details of it.

Coding a Windows Service requires several key pieces of information to function correctly and allow for proper deployment. In this chapter, we'll be building on the information we learned in Chapter 1, building another Windows Service, installing, and debugging it. This time we'll be building a monitoring service that monitors the World Wide Web Publishing Service. This service application will monitor at certain intervals and provide feedback via the Event Log as well as e-mail notification. Should the target service go down, our service application would attempt to restart it.

As well as implementing the functionality of the service, we'll look in more detail at:

- ❑ Service Security Contexts – the accounts a service can run under
- ❑ Service Logging Options – the different ways a service can inform the user what it is or isn't doing
- ❑ Service Installation
- ❑ Service Debugging

By the end of the chapter, we'll have another operable service and a deeper knowledge in the correct way to build and install a Windows Service either from Visual Studio .NET or from the command line.

Before we start building this new service, let's revise the code a service must have in order to function and how it works. As we know from Chapter 1, this translates to having another look at the `ServiceBase` class and the methods it defines that we'll have to override.

The ServiceBase Class

As we know, services are remotable, UI-less console applications that sit in a background process waiting for something to happen. We also know that all our service classes must derive from the .NET Windows Service base class, `System.ServiceProcess.ServiceBase`.

Looking at the bigger picture, the classes that `ServiceBase` derives confirm this description:

Figure 1

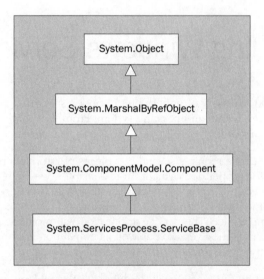

ServiceBase inherits from the `System.ComponentModel.Component` class, which contains the base implementation for an `IComponent` interface. This class is required by all applications that marshal by reference. The Component class is remotable and derives from the `System.MarshalByRefObject` class as seen in the illustration above.

Like most other console applications then, a service will begin executing instructions from its `Main()` method when it is started by the Service Control Manager. As described in the platform SDK, the SCM then waits for the service to call the `StartServiceCtrlDispatcher` API (located in `advapi32.lib`) before it does anything else. These steps still hark back to the days of service building with Visual C++ but, luckily for us, the .NET Framework does most of it automatically within the `ServiceBase` class.

Indeed, the default code for a Windows Service instantiates classes from the `ServiceBase` class automatically.

```
Shared Sub Main()
  Dim ServicesToRun() As System.ServiceProcess.ServiceBase
  ServicesToRun =
    New System.ServiceProcess.ServiceBase () {New Service1}
  System.ServiceProcess.ServiceBase.Run(ServicesToRun)
End Sub
```

Once you have a derived class, your `Main()` method must declare a `ServiceBase` object, which is passed the name of our service implementation class upon instantiation. `Main()` can then call `Run()` on the `ServiceBase` class and pass in the newly created `ServiceBase` object. So where's the call to the `StartServiceCtrlDispatcher` API mentioned earlier? Actually, it's handled transparently for us within `ServiceBase`.

By using ILDASM and examining the IL code of the `Run()` method within the `ServiceBase` class, we can see when and under what circumstances the `StartServiceCtrlDispatcher` is called for our service. The `Run()` method performs the following:

❑   The parameter of the `Run()` method is checked to ensure that it contains a valid `ServiceBase` object. If no parameter is provided, an error is thrown.

❑   `Environment.OSVersion.Platform` must return 2, or an error is thrown indicating that this project is not compatible with Win9X.

❑   If either of the previous two error conditions exists, `Run()` checks the `GetUserInteractive` method to see if someone is currently logged into the console. If so, an error message is displayed to the screen.

❑   If all conditions have been satisfied to this point, the `Run` method calls the `StartServiceCtrlDispatcher` with a pointer to the class within our service application. This method is external to the .NET Framework and is marshaled. This explains why the `ServiceBase` class inherits from the `Component` and `MarshalByRefObject` classes.

❑   Any resulting messages during the loading of this class will be either displayed on screen, written to the event log, or possibly both.

If the call to `StartServiceCtrlDispatcher` succeeds, the calling thread will not return until all the running threads within the process have terminated. This thread acts as a communications channel to the service and allows the Service Control Manager to send control requests to and from the service.

With the SCM ready to start the service, our service class should typically define at least four methods to get it running:

❑ In order to initialize any resources the service needs, we need to define its `OnStart` method. This must be declared as `Overrides` since it will replace the functionality the default code in `ServiceBase` provides. The base class also defines overridable methods for other events in a service's lifecycle, but, most importantly, `OnStop`, which we must also define to release the resources we created with `OnStart`.

❑ The service class typically also contains a constructor that makes a call to `InitializeComponent()`. Generally, this sets the name of the service as entered in the Properties window of the service project in Visual Studio. Calling this method is optional as you can assign this name directly in the constructor.

❑ The last method needed when creating a Windows Service is a `Dispose()` method. This method accepts one parameter, generally called `disposing`, of type `Boolean`. The `Dispose()` method overrides the base class and cleans up all objects in the project as well as all objects in the base class by using the `MyBase` keyword.

With that, it's time to put into practice what we've just learned.

Creating a Windows Service Project

The first step is to create a new VB.NET Windows Service project in Visual Studio .NET.

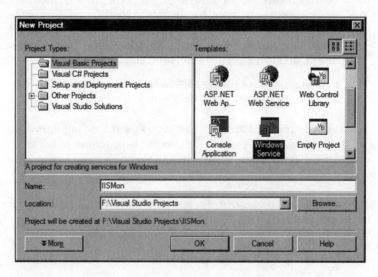

Since we will be building a service that actually monitors the Internet Information Server, let's call this new project IISMon. Technically, we're only concerned with one part of it – the World Wide Web Publishing service – but then again, how many of us actually use all of it? You probably don't use all of FTP, SMTP, and Web Services.

Once you've pressed OK, Visual Studio will churn out the basic code needed to start creating your Windows Service and open the design view for a file called Service1.vb. This is the main implementation file for our service and contains the class definition for the Windows Service application derived from System.ServiceProcess.ServiceBase. Right-click on the designer and select View Code to see this.

As we saw in Chapter 1, the service now has 99% of the functionality needed to run. We've no installer for it yet, but if we did and installed it, it would not do anything useful but it would run.

Service Properties

Just before we do give it something to do, let's make a few changes to the properties of this service and discover what they do. Double click on Service1.vb in the Solution Explorer, and the Properties window will display the various properties we can change for the service as a whole.

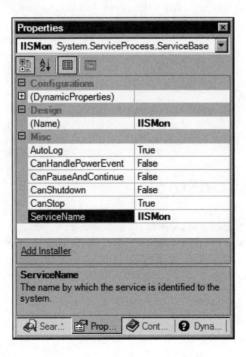

From top to bottom, the properties for a service are:

❏ Name

The name of the service class and the name you would use when starting and stopping it from the command line. Note that it needn't be the same name as the actual executable. Set it to `IISMon`.

❏ Autolog

Setting `AutoLog` to `True` enables the service to write entries to the Event Log for common events, such as when the service is installed, when it starts, and when it stops, to name just a few. Set this to `True`.

❏ CanHandlePowerEvent

Setting this property to `True` indicates that the service will receive messages about the power status of the machine. This proves useful when your service needs to know if the machine is currently preparing to power down or simply has a low battery. Set this to `False`.

❏ CanPauseAndContinue

Setting this to `True` means that instead of shutting down the service when it isn't needed, you have the option of pausing the service and then resuming it later. This relies on the `OnPause()` and `OnContinue()` methods. Set this to `False`.

❏ CanShutdown

Setting this property allows the service to know when the computer system is about to be shut down. Set this to `False`.

❏ CanStop

Determines if the service has to ability to stop once it has been started. Set this to `True`.

❏ ServiceName

The `ServiceName` is the name by which the Operating System identifies the service in the SCM and is identified in event logs. This is the short name for the service rather than the description. Set this to `IISMon`.

OnStart() and OnStop()

We've seen this before in Chapter 1, but it's worth noting again that VS.NET adds empty `OnStart()` and `OnStop()` methods to `Service1.vb`. If for some reason they haven't been make sure you add them manually. We'll add to them in due course.

```
Protected Overrides Sub OnStart(ByVal args() As String)

End Sub
```

```
Protected Overrides Sub OnStop()

End Sub
```

OnStart()'s string array argument will contain all of the parameters passed in when the service is started. As we've already discussed, a service cannot be started from a command prompt, unlike a typical executable, so typing in the name of the service followed by the parameters will result in an error message. The easiest way to pass parameters into a service is through the Service Control Manager, as we'll see later on.

Getting Your Service Talking Back

At last, we can move on to implementing the actual task we've set our service – reporting events in the WWW Publishing service. Seems simple enough, but how do we get IISMon to talk back to us?

Logging error messages and providing feedback on current service events is a little different from doing so in a typical application. A service has the unique ability to run in the background and with a different security context than a logged in user. If it happens that no user is currently logged into the machine, an attempt to display an error message would result in an exception being thrown and most likely the service would crash, With a service, you have to be more constructive, using the event logs, log files, e-mail notification, or perhaps even real time communications like Instant Messaging.

Event Log

By default, the System Event Log contains three logs to which messages are written – Security, System, and Application, where status and error messages are normally placed by applications, and where we'll place ours as well. We could create our own event log, but doing this would be overkill unless we had an extremely large application that would place numerous messages in the log.

Before we begin adding entries to the event log, we have a little setup work to do.

```
Public Class IISMon
    Inherits System.ServiceProcess.ServiceBase

    Private Const monInterval As Integer = 300
    Private Const svcName As String = "W3SVC"
    Private Const svcMachine As String = "Machine_Name"

    Private elEvents As New EventLog()
```

As you can see, we are declaring several constants and a new `EventLog` object, `elEvents`, for use throughout the service application.

- ❑ `monInterval` contains the number of seconds after which the service should poll IIS to determine if it is currently running or stopped.

- ❑ `svcName` contains the name of the service we will be checking for.

- ❑ `svcMachine` contains the name of the machine we are going to look at for this service status information. You'll need to modify this line to reflect your own server's name.

When the service starts we want it to write an entry in the event log detailing the poll interval. This we can do using `elEvents` in the service's `OnStart()` method:

```
Protected Overrides Sub OnStart(ByVal args() As String)
  elEvents.Source = "IISMon"
  elEvents.WriteEntry("IIS Monitor starting with an interval of " _
  & Me.monInterval.ToString() & " seconds.", _
  EventLogEntryType.Information)
End Sub
```

To achieve the required results, we need only do two things:

1. Set the `Source` property of the `EventLog` object to the name of the service application

2. Call the log's `WriteEntry()` method

The `WriteEntry()` method contains 10 overloaded versions, but the one typically used expects as parameters the message to write to the event log followed by any `EventLogEntryType` enumeration. The value of this enumeration defines the severity of the message within the event log. The enumeration values and a description of each are shown in the table below.

Value	Description
Error	This indicates an error condition that a user or systems administrator should be aware of. An `Error` entry generally means that there has been a loss of data or functionality.
FailureAudit	An entry type of `FailureAudit` generally happens after permission was denied for a particular operation. An example would be that your Windows Service application attempted to open a file and the request was denied.
Information	Informational messages generally refer to events that were successful as well as important.

Value	Description
SuccessAudit	This event type is generated when security permissions have been granted for a particular operation. For example, an administration application that controls your Windows Service would post a SuccessAudit when a user was granted permission to connect to the service and administer it.
Warning	Warnings are failures within the application or system. Typically, they don't need immediate attention but the problem that caused a warning could lead to an Error entry message being displayed.

One distinct advantage of using the System Event Log is that Windows itself has the ability to send certain types of notifications should a certain type of message show up in the event log. You could have Windows monitor the event log and if any errors show up for the IISMon service, you could have it send network pop-up messages. Apart from the functionality built into Windows, dozens of third-party applications permit a number of tasks to be performed based on Event Log activity.

Log File

Log files are another common method of reporting the status and general information from services, typically to a plain text file in a particular format such as CSV (Comma Separated Values). The advantage of using a log file is that you control everything about the format and location. You could make a new log file as frequently as you wish. You can code the log to rotate so it doesn't consume large amounts of drive space. An example of this type of file would be the log file that IIS generates. The log is generally named as <yymmdd>.log and stored in a secure location on the PC, such as a subdirectory of %WINNT%.

Using this type of logging, you could then import these custom logs into MS Excel or another tool later, to analyze the data. However, if you choose to stick with the System Event Log, that doesn't mean you can't report on the log information. The Event Viewer gives you the ability to export the information to any number of formats to import into external applications.

The disadvantage of creating your own log files is that you have to write the code to do everything, such as creating the log file, writing out the information, monitoring the file to ensure it doesn't get too big, as well as creating new log files at specified intervals if need be. It goes without saying that this can be rather time consuming. Unlike with the Event Log, there are no readily available tools able to monitor your log file and send notifications based on the content. Using tools like this on custom log files would force you to abide by certain formatting restrictions.

E-Mail

Reporting information using e-mail is very useful. Not only can you send e-mail to your home e-mail account or to your corporate helpdesk; with text pagers and digital cellular phones you can receive informational updates when you are anywhere in the world.

The .NET Framework provides two classes that make sending e-mail very simple. They are the `System.Web.Mail` class, which defines the mail message – who it's to, who it's from, the content, and its priority – and the `SmtpMail` class, which actually sends the message just created. If you wish to send an attachment with the e-mail you can also use the `MailAttachment` class to define the attachment for inclusion in the e-mail.

To demonstrate, we'll give IISMon the ability to send e-mail updates. First, we'll need to add a reference to `System.Web` in our project and import `System.Web.Mail` into our application and define a new constant containing the e-mail address to which all the e-mails will be sent. Don't forget to change this to your own e-mail address.

```
Imports System.ServiceProcess
Imports System.Web.Mail

Public Class Service1
    Inherits System.ServiceProcess.ServiceBase

    Private Const monInterval As Integer = 300
    Private Const svcName As String = "W3SVC"
    Private Const svcMachine As String = "Machine_Name"
    Private Const EmailTo As String = "me@my_email.com"
```

With that done we can add a simple method to our `IISMon` service class that sends an e-mail message to the predefined e-mail address.

```
    Private Sub SendEmail(ByVal MessageText As String)
        Dim ToSend As New MailMessage()

        ToSend.From = Me.ServiceName.ToString
        ToSend.To = Me.EmailTo
        ToSend.Subject = "IIS Service Status"
        ToSend.Priority = MailPriority.High
        ToSend.BodyFormat = MailFormat.Text
        ToSend.Body = MessageText
        SmtpMail.SmtpServer = "my.smtp.server"  'Change this
        SmtpMail.Send(ToSend)
    End Sub
```

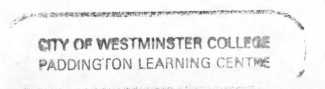

First we declare a new `MailMessage` object, set its `From` property to the name of our service and its `To` property to the e-mail address we declared earlier. We finish building the message by defining its subject line, priority, and the text format for the body and then send it. This needs us to supply a valid address for an SMTP server that IISMon can reach and then call `Send()`, passing the `MailMessage` object in as a parameter. Note that if you're running an NT-based system and have the SMTP service installed, you omit the value for the `SmtpServer` property. By doing so, the application will default to `localhost` for SMTP mail transmissions. Now we have a standalone method that accepts a string parameter as the message text that is then e-mailed to the specified e-mail address.

Since you probably don't want to be bothered by every little detail of the IISMon service, we will only call this function on two occasions; when the World Wide Web Publishing service (W3SVC) goes down and when it comes back up again. Details like the `IISMon` poll interval are better left in the System Event Log.

> Note that you could also set the e-mail address for the service from a
> .config file, rather than hardcode it into the service, for a little more
> flexibility. However, we'll leave this to the reader as an exercise.

Adding the Functionality

IISMon can now talk back at us, but currently it doesn't know when to do so. We've set an interval for its polling of W3SVC, but haven't introduced a way to count it down yet – a `Timer` object is a must have. Likewise, once the timer has counted down and W3SVC has been checked, we may need a way to attempt to restart it should we find it has stopped or been paused, and for that, we'll need a `ServiceController`.

Using a Timer

As we know, a `Timer` object will allow us to gauge the predetermined amount of time after which we check the status of the web service.

```
Public Class IISMon
    Inherits System.ServiceProcess.ServiceBase

    Private Const monInterval As Integer = 300
    Private Const svcName As String = "W3SVC"
    Private Const svcMachine As String = "Machine_Name"
    Private Const EmailTo As String = "me@my_email.com"

    Private cdTimer As System.Timers.Timer
    Private elEvents As New EventLog()
    Private NoticeSent As Boolean = False
    Private PeriodsDown As Long
```

What you might not know, however, is that the .NET Framework defines a few `Timer` objects, not all of them suited to our needs. The `System.Timers.Timer` object is considered a server-based timer. It is designed to work within multithreaded applications (like services) and has the ability to raise events on any thread within that application. On the other hand, the `System.Windows.Forms.Timer` object is a carry-over from previous versions of Visual Basic and is not capable of working in a multithreaded application. If we used this type of object in `IISMon`, it would cease to function correctly as soon as we began to test it.

You might ask why; we haven't added threads to this Windows Service project, and we haven't performed any specific thread programming at this point. The reason is simply that Visual Studio .NET has added the `MTAThread` attribute to our `Main()` method, which means all objects we use must be capable of running within a multithreaded (free-threaded) application.

> **So then, not only can we not use any UI-based components in a service, we now have to make sure that components are safe for use in a multi-threaded environment.**

We've also added two further `Private` variables to our service class, one for determining if an e-mail notice has been sent, and one to keep track of how long IIS is down. Now we can begin using the `Timer` object to poll IIS. All we need to do is get the `Timer` running once the service has been started. For that, we'll need to change `OnStart()` again.

```
Protected Overrides Sub OnStart(ByVal args() As String)

    ' Create a timer object with specified interval
    cdTimer = New Timers.Timer(Me.monInterval * 1000)
    ' Add an event handler for our new timer.
    AddHandler cdTimer.Elapsed, AddressOf Me.OnTimerElapsed
    cdTimer.Start()
    elEvents.Source = "IISMon"
    elEvents.WriteEntry("IIS Monitor starting with an interval of " _
        & Me.monInterval.ToString() & " seconds.", _
        EventLogEntryType.Information)
End Sub
```

Before we can start the Timer, we need to create it and then set out what needs to happen once it's finished counting down.

The standard constructor for `System.Timers.Timer` takes the interval it's measuring as a parameter, given in milliseconds. The above code then, sets up our service to poll IIS every 300 seconds (5 minutes). The `Timer` object now knows when to fire, but we need to add an event handler to specify the method to call when the period has elapsed. We use `AddHandler` to make it call our own function, `OnTimerElapsed`, at the appropriate time.

```
Private Sub OnTimerElapsed( _
            ByVal sender As Object, _
            ByVal e As System.Timers.ElapsedEventArgs)
End Sub
```

We'll be using this method to create our event log messages and send our e-mails in a while, but before we do, there's the matter of actually polling IIS to see what it's doing. For that, we need to make use of a `ServiceController` object.

Using a ServiceController

The `ServiceController` object allows us to check the status of a currently registered service, start the service, stop it, and even control its overall behavior.

```
Private cdTimer As Timers.Timer
Private elEvents As New EventLog()
Private SvcControl As ServiceController
Private NoticeSent As Boolean = False
Private PeriodsDown As Long
```

Once we've declared a `ServiceController` object, we can use it to check the status of the IIS Service once the Timer has elapsed.

```
Private Sub OnTimerElapsed( _
    ByVal sender As Object, _
    ByVal e As System.Timers.ElapsedEventArgs)
  Me.SvcControl = New ServiceController(Me.svcName, Me.svcMachine)
  If Me.SvcControl.Status = ServiceControllerStatus.Stopped Then

  End If
End Sub
```

To instantiate a new `ServiceController` object, we need to pass it the name of the service we're working with and the name of the machine where the service is located. (As long as you know the name of the service then, you could use this code to check the status of any service on any server on your LAN.) With this done, checking the service's status is a matter of checking the `Status` property of the `ServiceController` and comparing it to the `ServiceControllerStatus` enumeration defined in `System.ServiceProcess`. The table overleaf details the possible results of the check of the `Status` property.

Status Message	Description
ContinuePending	The service is currently Paused but is in the process of resuming its normal operations.
Paused	The service is paused and no longer executing instructions.
PausePending	The service is currently running but a pause request was issued. The OnPause() method is running and when completed, the service will be in a Paused state.
Running	The service is currently running normally.
StartPending	The service is in the process of starting up.
Stopped	The service has been stopped, either by a command from a user or because it suffered a fatal error and was shut down.
StopPending	The service is currently running but is in the process of stopping. Once the OnStop() method has finished executing, the service will stop and unload from memory.

It is important to know that when you use a
ServiceController object, you have the option of using the
Refresh method to update status information concerning the
service, rather than creating a new ServiceController each
time. In this example, we have chosen to create a new object
each time. This reduces the memory footprint by creating
the object only when it is needed and letting it be removed
when garbage collection determines it isn't.

Now that we are able to determine if the service has been stopped we can begin
adding code to send an e-mail notification, log the information in the Event Log, and
attempt to restart the service.

```
Private Sub OnTimerElapsed( _
 ByVal sender As Object, _
 ByVal e As System.Timers.ElapsedEventArgs)

  Me.SvcControl = New ServiceController(Me.svcName, Me.svcMachine)
  If Me.SvcControl.Status = ServiceControllerStatus.Stopped Then
      ' Increment our counter so we can track how many times
      ' this service has been down
      PeriodsDown += 1

      If NoticeSent = False Then
         elEvents.Source = "IISMon"
```

```
        elEvents.WriteEntry("IIS is currently down", _
           EventLogEntryType.Warning)

        SendEmail("IIS is currently down on server " & svcMachine)

        NoticeSent = True
      End If

      ' Attempt to start the service
      Me.SvcControl.Start()

   Else

      If NoticeSent = True Then
         elEvents.Source = "IISMon"
         elEvents.WriteEntry("IIS is currently running", _
         EventLogEntryType.Information)

         SendEmail("IIS is currently running on server " & svcMachine)
         ' Clear our flag.
         NoticeSent = False
      End If
    End If
 End Sub
```

The service is now fully functional. It will poll the IIS Service every five minutes. If the service goes down, it will log an event to the Event Log, send an e-mail notification, and then attempt to restart the service. At the next poll interval, if the service has come back up when it was previously down – another e-mail will be sent.

Creating a Service Installer

Of course, if we want to use the service, we need to build an installer for it before we can set it off. We've already seen that VS.NET will do most of this for us if we ask, but what is it actually creating?

In Visual Studio .NET, double-click Service1.vb again, and then double-click the hyperlink reading Add Installer in the Properties window. A new file, ProjectInstaller.vb, is created containing instances of two objects – a ServiceInstaller and a ServiceProcessInstaller. Both these objects are needed by the installation utility to actually register the service in the Windows registry and install the executable for use.

❏   The ServiceInstaller does the majority of the work, adding registry entries as required. The properties for this object also define the name of the service (ServiceName) and the name displayed within the Service Control Manager (DisplayName). ServiceInstallers work on a one-to-one basis with their service, so if your project contains multiple services, you'll need an equal number of ServiceInstallers.

❏   The `ServiceProcessInstaller` encapsulates all the
        `ServiceInstaller` objects, and it is only needed once within a Windows
        Service application project.

To create these objects without the use of Visual Studio .NET, create a
`ProjectInstaller` class that inherits from
`System.Configuration.Install.Installer`. This class should have a
`RunInstaller` attribute set to `True` for things to work correctly. Within this class, you
will need to instantiate one `ServiceProcessInstaller` instance and one
`ServiceInstaller` instance per service within the assembly. You then add both of
these objects to the `Installers` collection, which is provided by the base class.

Of course, if you are using VS.NET, the code is automatically generated for us in
ProjectInstaller.vb. It is shown here for reference purposes.

```
Imports System.ComponentModel
Imports System.Configuration.Install
```

When you run a service installation utility, it looks though the assembly for a
`RunInstaller` attribute that is set to `True`. When it finds this attribute, it installs the
services that are located within the `Installers` collection.

```
<RunInstaller(True)> Public Class ProjectInstaller
  Inherits System.Configuration.Install.Installer

  Public Sub New()
    MyBase.New()
    InitializeComponent()
  End Sub

  Protected Overloads Overrides Sub Dispose( _
                            ByVal disposing As Boolean)
    If disposing Then
      If Not (components Is Nothing) Then
        components.Dispose()
      End If
    End If
    MyBase.Dispose(disposing)
  End Sub

  Private components As System.ComponentModel.IContainer

  Friend WithEvents ServiceProcessInstaller1 As _
    System.ServiceProcess.ServiceProcessInstaller
  Friend WithEvents ServiceInstaller1 As _
    System.ServiceProcess.ServiceInstaller
  <System.Diagnostics.DebuggerStepThrough()> _
  Private Sub InitializeComponent()
```

```
      Me.ServiceProcessInstaller1 = New _
        System.ServiceProcess.ServiceProcessInstaller()
      Me.ServiceInstaller1 = New _
        System.ServiceProcess.ServiceInstaller()

      Me.ServiceProcessInstaller1.Account = _
        System.ServiceProcess.ServiceAccount.LocalSystem
      Me.ServiceProcessInstaller1.Password = Nothing
      Me.ServiceProcessInstaller1.Username = Nothing

      Me.ServiceInstaller1.DisplayName = "IIS Monitor"
      Me.ServiceInstaller1.ServiceName = "IISMon"

      Me.Installers.AddRange( _
        New System.Configuration.Install.Installer() _
        {Me.ServiceProcessInstaller1, Me.ServiceInstaller1})
    End Sub
  End Class
```

We noted earlier that the `ServiceInstaller's` `DisplayName` property is what we see when we start looking at installed services in the Microsoft Management Console. (The SCM is an MMC snap-in.) What we don't see is the name we give to the service class. So then, let's give our service a more appropriate name. Select the `ServiceInstaller` object in VS.NET and change its `DisplayName` property to "IIS Monitor".

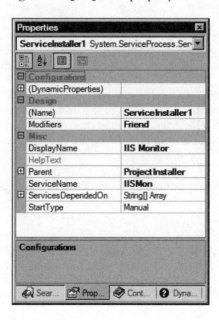

Setting the DisplayName property to something more meaningful helps a great deal when you are looking at a list of Services in the MMC. Not everyone will know by seeing IISMon what your service actually does. The fact it shows IIS Monitor instead greatly reduces any assumptions that could be made about the service. If you have more information you'd like to provide with this service, the MMC also provides a Description field for this use.

We'll now move on to security contexts, which define what kind of permissions your service is granted.

Service Security Contexts

Service Security Contexts indicate the level of privilege a service has on the system and how the service interacts with other systems on the network. We can define this context for a service, by giving its ServiceProcessInstaller one of four enumerated values of type ServiceAccount for its Account property, as you saw in the previous chapter:

- ❑ User
- ❑ LocalService
- ❑ LocalSystem
- ❑ NetworkService

It might appear more obvious to define the security context as a property of the service itself, but the installer needs the information, not the service. When you install your service, the installer must know for what kind of logon to configure the service.

If your service is to use an account that you have created on the local machine or domain, you must provide that information to the installer so the service can log in when it needs to. On the other hand, you may choose a security context that has predefined security attributes and so doesn't require user intervention during the installation process.

Let's look at the possible ServiceAccount members available before settling with one for the IISMon service.

User

The User ServiceAccount is the default when creating a Windows Service. This lets us specify the username of an account on the local machine or on a domain controller under whose account the service will run. As noted in Chapter 1, if this option is used, the service installer will prompt you for that login information during the installation itself.

If that's perhaps a bit risky in your work environment, you can specify a username and password within the installer itself so it won't ask for this information explicitly. To accomplish this, you simply need to set the UserName and Password properties of the ServiceProcessInstaller object in our ProjectInstaller class. For example,

```
Me.ServiceProcessInstaller1.Account =
                 System.ServiceProcess.ServiceAccount.User
Me.ServiceProcessInstaller1.Password = "LETMEIN"
Me.ServiceProcessInstaller1.Username = "POWERHOUSE\Brian"
```

Obviously, you wouldn't want to code a valid username and password into your application because it poses a serious security concern. The proper thing to do would be to use dummy information that would allow the service to install uninterrupted and then remind the user to change this information through the Service Control Manager after the installation has completed.

We won't be using this type of security in our service so let's move on. The other three security contexts don't require you to enter in logon information either, and have the extra advantage that the extent of their privileges can be controlled at the machine or domain level by use of the Security Settings Management Console.

LocalService

The LocalService type has almost complete access to the machine on which the service is running. If your service needs information from across the network, the LocalService will present its credentials to other servers for this purpose. If your service is running on a machine that has a trust relationship with the other servers on the network, this will allow your service access to these network resources.

Specify this as your account type timidly. LocalService has administrative access to the machine where the service runs, and quite possibly to other machines on your network. If you use this context type for a production service application, it would be wise to implement code access security in case someone should exploit a bug in your code to gain access to the system.

Remember that it's always best to grant the least amount of permissions the application needs. To run IISMon as LocalService would be overkill so let's move on.

LocalSystem

LocalSystem is almost the opposite of LocalService. It runs as an unprivileged user on the machine, and it will present anonymous credentials to all servers requesting information. Though LocalSystem doesn't have much access, it does provide enough for this service. Set the Account property of the ServiceProcessInstaller to LocalSystem as seen overleaf:

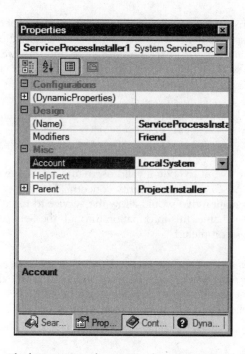

When we are done with this service, the main advantage it has is that not only will it monitor when the Web Publishing Service goes down but it will then attempt to restart it. You may come to realize that if you are using IISMon to monitor a remote server, your attempt to restart the service, should it go down, will fail. This is because LocalSystem doesn't have the access to remote servers like that of LocalService. If you encounter this problem, simply change this property to User and create a local user account IISMon can use. You also have the option of changing this property to LocalService but keep in mind that this could have security implications if you are in a corporate network environment. The example we are building here assumes that you have IIS installed on the same machine that IISMon is running.

LocalSystem is a typical local user to the machine. There is no direct access to ports less than 1024 nor is there access to the registry and other secure locations within the operating system.

NetworkService

NetworkService is a combination of the previous security contexts. It is an unprivileged user for the service, yet when a remote server requests credentials, NetworkService responds with the credentials of the local machine. Therefore, it may not have many permissions, but it does identify itself to remote servers. Like LocalSystem, it also has no direct access to ports less than 1024 nor is there access to the registry and other secure locations within the operating system.

(Un)Installing the Service

We've finally reached the point where the service does everything we want it to and will install itself in the SCM without a hitch. Now we need to test it. We've seen how to build and install a service before, so we'll run through it quickly.

❏   In VS.NET, select Build | Build Solution or press *Ctrl + Shift + B*.

❏   Open a VS.NET Command Prompt Window from the Start Menu.

❏   Now navigate to My Documents\IISMon\bin.

❏   Type InstallUtil IISMon.exe to install and register your application as a Windows Service. After a few seconds, you'll be told the service has installed successfully.

The process of uninstalling the service is very similar. Follow the first three steps for installation and then

❏   Type InstallUtil /u IISMon.exe to uninstall the service. After a dew seconds, you'll be told the service has uninstalled successfully.

As you can probably tell, the /u parameter means uninstall. There are also command-line switches to view the call stack, log all information to a particular file, and for many other useful options. For a list of options look at InstallUtil.Exe in the MSDN documentation, or type installutil /? from a console window.

> *Note that it is possible to uninstall a service while it is running. If the installation tool determines that the service is running, it will stop the service before it uninstalls it.*

Installing a Service Remotely

Deploying this or any other Windows Service to a machine other than where it was developed is a very easy task. Once you have compiled the application and have an executable, you need only copy the executable to the target machine. The target machine must contain the Microsoft .NET Framework, either the full SDK or the redistributable version. Once you have copied the executable there you simply use the installation utility to install and register the service.

In Chapter 7 we will cover using Visual Studio .NET to create a deployment project capable of installing all necessary files as well as automating the installation with the provided installation tool.

Testing the Service

To test the service, we'll need to get it up and running once it's been installed.

❑ Right-click on My Computer and choose Manage.

❑ When the MMC window opens, expand the Services and Applications item in the left pane and select Services.

❑ You'll see the IISMon service listed in the right-hand window pane, as seen here:

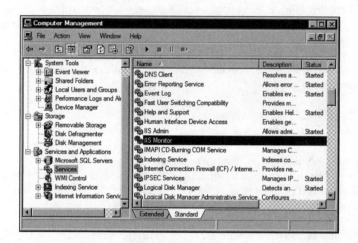

❑ To start the service, right-click on it and Choose Start. The value in the Status column will change from blank to Started.

You can also start the service from a console window by typing Net start and then the name of the service.

> **Net start IISMon**

If you start the service this way, a message will be displayed indicating if the service was started successfully.

Now the service has been installed and it is running, stop the IIS service to ensure the application works correctly. Stop the W3SVC service, either from the Management Console or from a console window (by typing Net stop W3SVC). Depending on how long ago IISMon was started, you may have to wait up to five minutes before seeing any results. After a few minutes, check your Event Viewer, which also happens to be in the Management Console. In the Application log, you should see an event with a source of IISMon saying that the service was started successfully. You should also see an event that tells you how often it will poll IIS for status information.

Once five minutes has elapsed, you should see an entry saying that IIS is currently down. Shortly after this event appears, you should receive an e-mail as well. Recall that if IIS goes down, the service will issue a `Start` request. At the next poll interval, you should see another Event Log entry stating that the IIS service has been started – as well as an e-mail.

Once you are sure everything is working, you can stop the service. From the Management Console, or a console window, stop the `IISMon` service. Once you have stopped the `IISMon` service, you should see two additional Event Log entries. One should say that the service was stopped and the other should contain a message detailing how long IIS was down. Remember that this time can be off considerably since the service only polls every 5 minutes. It's likely that IIS was restarted immediately after the request was issued, yet we don't know that until the `IISMon` service checks the status of IIS five minutes later.

If you wish to make any coding changes to the `IISMon` services, you must stop it from running first. If the service is running when you try to compile a new version, you will receive an error message since the Executable is in use and cannot be replaced.

Debugging the Service

As you have already seen, debugging a Windows Service is a little trickier than with a typical application. Since you can't simply run a Windows Service in Visual Studio by pressing *F5*, you obviously can't step through it and set break points.

Not to worry, however, because the Visual Studio environment provides you with the tools you need to effectively debug a Windows Service process.

Process Attachment

Process attachment allows you to connect Visual Studio, and the source code you are currently working with, to a process that is currently running on the local machine or across the network on a remote machine. If you uninstalled the IISMon service as we did in the previous section, you will need to reinstall it before you'll be able to debug it.

To begin debugging the Windows Service, ensure that the service is running, click on the Tools menu, and choose Debug Processes. A list of all currently running processes is displayed, as well as the process types and process IDs. A Windows Service is a system process, so ensure that the Show system processes checkbox is checked. Once you have located the `IISMon` process, click the Attach button. You must then select the program types that you wish to debug. Check the box next to Common Language Runtime and click the OK button. You will then be returned to the process list where you can click the Close button.

To test things out, click the Debug menu and choose Break All. It will pause the currently running process and let you set break points and anything you need to do. Scroll through your code and locate the first If condition in the Timer elapsed event. Set a break point on this line by clicking on it and pressing *F9*. A red dot will appear denoting a break point; now we can resume the process by pressing *F5*.

```
        SmtpMail.Send(ToSend)
    End Sub

    Private Sub OnTimerElapsed( _
            ByVal sender As Object, _
            ByVal e As System.Timers.ElapsedEventArgs)
        Me.SvcControl = New ServiceController(Me.svcName, Me.svcMachine)
        If Me.SvcControl.Status = ServiceControllerStatus.Stopped Then
            ' Increment our counter so we can track how many times
            ' this service has been down
            PeriodsDown += 1

            ' We need to determine if a notice has already been sent
            ' to the email address.  If so, there is no point in
            ' sending another one.
            If NoticeSent = False Then
```

After five minutes has elapsed, Visual Studio should break in the process and highlight the line with the breakpoint set. You can now step through the code by pressing *F11* to move one line of code at a time. If need be, you can change the constant value monInterval to something more reasonable such as 30 seconds so you don't have to wait five minutes for the breakpoint to be reached.

```
    End Sub

    Private Sub OnTimerElapsed( _
            ByVal sender As Object, _
            ByVal e As System.Timers.ElapsedEventArgs)
        Me.SvcControl = New ServiceController(Me.svcName, Me.svcMachine)
        If Me.SvcControl.Status = ServiceControllerStatus.Stopped Then
            ' Increment our counter so we can track how many times
            ' this service has been down
            PeriodsDown += 1

            ' We need to determine if a notice has already been sent
            ' to the email address.  If so, there is no point in
            ' sending another one.
```

After you have completed debugging the service process, you need to return to the Process list by going to the tools menu or by pressing *Ctrl+Alt+P*. Once there, select the process at the bottom of the window and click the Detach button. This will ensure that the Windows Service continues to run, whereas clicking the Terminate button or stopping debugging within Visual Studio would shut the Windows Service down.

Failsafe

Adding a failsafe to your service is a way of saying that you'll use structured error handling. Rather than performing operations that you hope will succeed, wrap statements throughout your application in Try-Catch blocks. This ensures that if an operation fails, you can safely recover from the error, report the error if need be, and continue.

If an unhandled exception occurs within a Windows Service application, the service will simply exit with no warning or message stating why it quit. In the example service created above, the most logical place for structured error handling would be around the `ServiceController` object. This would ensure that if the service does not exist, or perhaps if the network is down, the service wouldn't simply quit.

The following code illustrates the adding of a failsafe:

```
Private Sub OnTimerElapsed( _
     ByVal sender As Object, _
     ByVal e As System.Timers.ElapsedEventArgs)
  Try
     Me.SvcControl = New ServiceController(Me.svcName, Me.svcMachine)
  Catch se As Exception
     elEvents.Source = "IISMon"
     elEvents.WriteEntry(se.Message, EventLogEntryType.Warning)

     SendEmail(se.Message)
     Exit Sub
  End Try
```

As you can see from this code, we try to instantiate a new `ServiceController` object. If this operation fails, we write an event log message and send an e-mail. Both of these options use the `Message` property of the exception when reporting the error condition. After the messages have been sent, we simply exit the method by calling `Exit Sub`. There isn't any point in attempting to resume the method since the `ServiceController` failed. Something like this might happen if the machine where the service resides is down, you may have entered in an incorrect service name, or network problems may exist that are preventing you from reaching a remote server – to name a few.

Summary

In this chapter, we've expanded on the issues and objects involved in coding a full-blown Windows Service that we first saw in Chapter 1. In particular, we've looked in more detail at:

- ❑ The `ServiceBase` class from which all service classes must be derived

- ❑ Why some .NET components will not work within a Windows Service – they are not appropriate for a multithreaded environment

- ❑ The different means we have of getting our service to report its progress

- ❑ The function of the `ServiceInstaller` and `ServiceProcessInstaller` objects

❏   The four security contexts that we can set up our service to run under

❏   The idea of failsafe code

We have also revised the procedures needed to build, install, start, test, debug, stop, and uninstall a service. In the next chapter, you'll learn about the various methods to configure and control Windows Services.

VB.NET

Windows Services

Handbook

4

4

Configuring and Controlling Windows Services

While Windows Services can be built that are simply installed, started, and left to run in the background, all but the most trivial services will offer some form of configurability, or facility for receiving and processing commands. In this chapter, we'll look at some of the options that exist for Windows Services to load configuration information when they are started, or to respond to commands while they are running. We'll see how this enables us to create services that can be maintained by a server administrator using familiar Windows and web interfaces, and how it also allows us to write user-space Windows programs that can interact with and control running services.

This chapter will cover the following:

- ❏ Basic control of services
- ❏ Configuration of services
- ❏ Issuing commands to services
- ❏ Developing a Windows Service GUI
- ❏ Using WMI to control and monitor services

Mechanisms for Controlling Services

Windows Services themselves, as we know, have no direct graphical interface. They run as background services, usually under the context of a privileged user. However, with many services it is essential that they have an interface for controlling their behavior. This control mechanism can be as simple as the management snap-in provided in Windows to control Windows Services. This will enable the administrator of the service to control the service's common behavior such as starting, stopping, pausing, and resuming the service and provide some basic configuration alternatives. This model of using common, basic tools such as the services snap-in to control service behavior may be sufficient for some services. Others will need a greater level of control, which may involve extra-functionality provided by the service, which will need to be configured. It's possible to build our service so that it responds to other commands apart from the basic start, stop, and pause; we'll see how later in this chapter.

A variety of GUI applications exist that allow us to interact with services. Examples of these are the IIS and SQL Server snap-ins in the Microsoft Management Console. The MMC allows 'snap-ins' to be written to allow a standard control interface for an application – this interface will be familiar to most administrators and can be customized to contain a multitude of snap-ins for a range of applications so that the console can be used as a single point of management for the system. All of the tools under the Administrative tools menu of Windows 2000 server are written as MMC snap-ins.

We can develop a GUI in any environment – not just the MMC – that controls or configures a service, but we need a way to communicate from the GUI application to the service. IIS offers one solution to this problem. We can generally interact with the IIS **metabase** (that is, the data that constitutes IIS's configuration) through the Active Directory Services Interface, ADSI. ADSI provides a standard programmatic interface to a variety of applications; it is most notably used to configure IIS and configure security and management in Windows, as well as for applications such as Commerce Server. By writing an application that accesses the IIS metabase, we can recreate the effect of the IIS MMC snap-in using a different GUI. The important point here is that well designed applications such as IIS and SQL Server expose their functionality to allow configuration and control – whether it be through an ADSI interface or the SQL interface we can use to amend the system tables in SQL Server.

WMI (Windows Management Instrumentation, which we will examine later in the chapter) also allows programmatic control and configuration of Windows Services (and applications and operating system components generally). Similarly we can generally issue commands via message passing if the service contains a network listener; this can be done through any form of protocol (e.g. HTTP and SMTP use simple single worded commands) In this way we can develop a web page or a Windows form that can be used to control the application and to change various configuration parameters (as we will see later these options are generally far less of a development headache than developing an MMC snap-in!).

Basic Control through the SCM

As we've seen before, all services' lifecycles are controlled through the **Service Control Manager (SCM)**, which starts and stops service processes, and generally keeps order among services.

We can exercise basic control over the behavior of our service through the SCM. As we'll see, the SCM also provides a programmatic interface through which we can examine, start, and stop registered services from within our own code. But first, let's look at a couple of the advanced features the SCM supports for service startup and shutdown, and error recovery.

Service Recovery

Each service allows recovery to be enabled such that if the service process crashes then the SCM will be monitoring the service and restart it. There is a fine-grained level of recovery for the service, which enables rules to be set for the first, second, and third times that the service crashes.

The recovery aspect of a service can be configured through the service property pages, which will enable the SCM to monitor the behavior of the service such that if the service crashes and a stop is forced by the SCM then it will be immediately restarted.

The service control manager can be configured to:

- ❏ Take no action
- ❏ Restart the service
- ❏ Restart the computer
- ❏ Execute a program

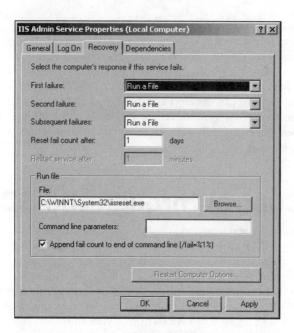

There is a high level of control over the recovery parameters. Delays can be set for starting the recovery program or for restarting the system. (A message can also be broadcast to terminals on the network before the reboot takes place.) Recovery such as this can be fantastic for ensuring that services will be fault tolerant and reliable. For example, if an ISAPI application causes the IISAdmin service to crash (if running in low process isolation) then the service will automatically run a program called iisreset.exe, which will ensure that the service process is restarted (and the web server will have little downtime as a result).

Service Dependencies

A service can be reliant on other services in order to function. In this instance it is said to have dependencies, which allow startup of the service to be conditional upon those services being available. To give an example, later in this chapter we will develop an application as a Windows Service, which will access a SQL Server database and convert relational data into a set of XML files. This service would not be able to function without SQL Server and will return an immediate connection error if the SQL server is not present (assuming that the application was created to access a local SQL Server instance). If the SQL server is not present and it was marked as a service dependency then the XMLData service we were trying to start would fail (the SCM would return an exception) during startup – before we reach the problem in our own code. Similarly, by marking another service as a dependency, we can generally ensure that if the SQL Server service is in a stopped state when the XMLData service is started then it will be started. One less thing to worry about or check for in our own service code!

Here's the service dependencies property page for the IISAdmin service:

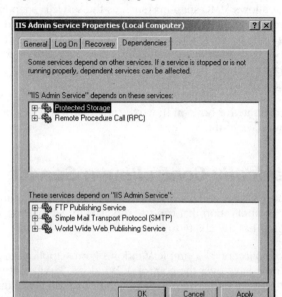

SCM Interfaces

Every service can be started and stopped via the SCM through a variety of means. We've already used the service property pages (shown above) to stop, start, or pause services but this may not always be appropriate. During many applications installations, services may need to be stopped. This (as we'll see later in the chapter) can be done in several ways programmatically. We can also use the command line to do this which will allow for easy scripting in a batch file.

In order to stop the IISAdmin service, for example, we can use:

```
> net stop IISAdmin
```

You'll normally be asked if you want to stop the dependent services. This can be avoided by following the command with a /Y switch. In either case, ultimately, this will shut down the IISAdmin service, and its dependent services such as w3svc (the WWW Service)

Correspondingly we can use net start IISAdmin to restart the service, but note that this won't start the dependent services. Starting the WWW Service (w3svc) instead, however, will start up the service on which it depends (IISAdmin), as well as the w3svc service itself.

It is worth mentioning at this point that MMCv2 that comes with Windows XP expose an object model that allows MMC snap-ins (such as the services snap-in) to be controlled programmatically. This allows VBScript files to be run through the WSH (Windows scripting host) to allow scripted control of the MMC. This chapter will not contain details of the control interfaces but more information can be found in the March Issue of MSDN magazine here:
http://msdn.microsoft.com/msdnmag/issues/01/03/mmc20/mmc20.asp.

We're going to concentrate for now on how we can control services programmatically, through the .NET interface to the SCM.

Programmatically Controlling a Service

Before looking at how we can configure services during installation time and startup time we'll describe an application that can use the SCM to get information on all registered services and has the ability to control the services.

The `AllServices` application is a simple Windows Forms application that illustrates the power that we now have over the control of Windows Services. It will use the `System.ServiceProcess` namespace to retrieve information about the service and issue commands to the SCM to enable the service to be stopped, started, paused or continued from a pause command. We met the `ServiceController` class briefly in the previous chapter, but now we'll have a chance to see what it can really do.

The application is simple enough, consisting of one main form, `Services.vb`, and a form we use to display information, `Supplementary.vb`. Here's the design for `Services.vb`:

The big central pane is a listbox, called `lbServiceItems`. The buttons across the bottom are called, from left to right: `btStart`, `btStop`, `btPause`, and `btGetServices`. The Start, Stop, and Pause buttons are all disabled to begin with – they'll be enabled as appropriate once a list of services has been retrieved.

Here's `SupplementaryInfo.vb`:

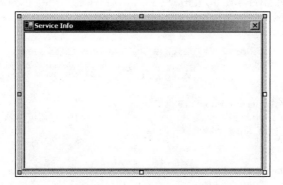

It contains a single large, multiline textbox, called `txtServiceInfo`.

All the application code is in the `Services.vb` source file, which begins with the following imports:

```
Imports System
Imports System.ServiceProcess
Imports System.Collections
Imports System.Text
```

Within the `Services` form class, the declarations include a structure that will hold both the display name and the service name of a service. This is necessary since the `ServiceController` class can only reference services through their service names rather than their display names. However, the user will want to see the service's display name. This structure provides a convenient means for us to store both.

```
'This struct holds the display and service names
   Private Structure Names
      Dim displayName As String
      Dim serviceName As String
   End Structure
```

Two member variables are also needed to hold the service whose display name is currently selected in the listbox and an `ArrayList` to hold a collection of `Names` structures.

```
'holds all the names of all the services
   Private nameHolder As New ArrayList()
```

```
'holds the currently selected service
Private currentService As New ServiceController()
'holds a Boolean value indicating if we're currently showing devices
or services
Private m_Services As Boolean = False
```

The first action will always be to retrieve a list of services. When the Get Services List button is clicked the following code will be invoked:

```
Private Sub btGetServices_Click(ByVal sender As System.Object, _
                        ByVal e As System.EventArgs) _
              Handles btGetServices.Click

    Dim scm As ServiceController()
    Dim i As Integer = 0
    Dim isServices As Boolean = True

    nameHolder.Clear()
    lbServiceItems.Items.Clear()
    If Not m_Services Then
      isServices = False
      m_Services = True
    Else
      m_Services = False
    End If
```

As we've described in Chapter 2 there are different types of services managed by the SCM. Through our code we can retrieve a list of application services or device driver services using different methods of the ServiceController class. We check the state of the member variable m_Services – this will hold a Boolean value indicating whether the current request is for Windows application services or for device driver services. The ServiceController methods GetServices() and GetDevices(), both instance methods, are called to retrieve the list.

```
    'If left blank this will retrieve all the local services
    If isServices Then
      scm = currentService.GetServices()
    Else
      scm = currentService.GetDevices()
    End If
```

The last thing that remains is to extract the display names of the services from the ServiceController array we generated in the above code and add the display name to the listbox. Following this the Names structure must be populated with the display name and the service name and added to the nameHolder ArrayList. The order that the names are shown in the listbox is the same order in which the ArrayList holds the collection of Names structures.

```
While (i < scm.Length - 1)
  lbServiceItems.Items.Add(scm(i).DisplayName)
  Dim n As Names
  n.displayName = scm(i).DisplayName
  n.serviceName = scm(i).ServiceName
  nameHolder.Add(n)
  i = i + 1
End While
```

So, we've populated the listbox with service names, and we have a list of Names structures we can use to associate each item in the list with a service name. We need to configure the user interface so that the user is now presented with the correct options:

```
butGetServices.Text = "Get Services List"
If isServices Then butGetServices.Text = "Get Device List"
End Sub
```

The other buttons will remain disabled until a service is selected from the list. This is indicated to our code when the listbox raises a SelectedIndexChanged event. Here's our handler:

```
Private Sub lbServiceItems_SelectedIndexChanged( _
                        ByVal sender As Object, _
                        ByVal e As EventArgs) _
            Handles lbServiceItems.SelectedIndexChanged
```

In order to control the application GUI and to ensure that only appropriate commands are issued to a·highlighted service we have to check the service status. Status reflects the current state of the service – it is a response to an SCM request as to whether the service is stopped or started, etc. Services can be subject to irregular behavior and a stop or start pending state can be issued when the service has "hung" – this state can continue indefinitely in some circumstances.

Our first task then is to identify the name of the service the user selected. We obtain the SelectedIndex of the listbox and retrieve the service name of the selected service by looking up the corresponding Names structure in the list. A ServiceController object is created by passing in this string. This results in a ServiceController instance for the service.

```
Dim localService As New ServiceController( _
            DirectCast(nameHolder(lbServiceItems.SelectedIndex), _
            Names).serviceName)
```

In order to test the status of the service we can check the status property and use the ServiceControllerStatus enumeration. This will enable the buttons to be disabled or in the case of the Pause button, the button text to be changed.

The `ServiceController` enumeration defines the following values.

❑   `ContinuePending`

❑   `Paused`

❑   `PausePending`

❑   `Running`

❑   `StartPending`

❑   `Stopped`

❑   `StopPending`

We've listed these values because it is important to differentiate between the pending states and the definite states. The **pending** state will occur while a process is trying to stop or start or pause-continue a service. Our application can detect this status and change its behavior accordingly. We'll only allow the user to issue commands if the service is definitely in one of these states.

```
Select Case localService.Status
  Case ServiceControllerStatus.Stopped
    btStop.Enabled = False
    btStart.Enabled = True
    btPause.Enabled = False
  Case ServiceControllerStatus.Running
    btStop.Enabled = True
    btStart.Enabled = False
    btPause.Enabled = True
    btPause.Text = "Pause"
  Case ServiceControllerStatus.Paused
    btStop.Enabled = True
    btStart.Enabled = False
    btPause.Enabled = True
    btPause.Text = "Continue"
  Case Else
    btStop.Enabled = False
    btStart.Enabled = False
    btPause.Enabled = False
  End Select
End Sub
```

The `Click` event on each button is handled by almost identical methods, which try to perform the relevant action on the highlighted service. The `CheckHighlighted` function ensures that a value has been highlighted in the listbox – if this were not the case then the `localService` variable would contain a null reference.

```
Private Function CheckHighlighted() As Boolean
  If lbServiceItems.SelectedIndex = -1 Then
    Return False
  Else
    Return True
  End If
End Function
```

Here's the stop button's click handler:

```
Private Sub btStop_Click(ByVal sender As System.Object, _
                  ByVal e As System.EventArgs) _
              Handles btStop.Click
  Dim localService As New ServiceController( _
            DirectCast(nameHolder(lbServiceItems.SelectedIndex), _
            Names).serviceName)

  If CheckHighlighted() Then
    Try
      localService.Stop()
    Catch ex As Exception
      MessageBox.Show(ex.Message)
    End Try
  End If
End Sub
```

When an item in the listbox is double-clicked the lbServiceItems_DoubleClick event handler is invoked. This creates and focuses a new form that contains information about the highlighted service. The following code makes up the method:

```
Private Sub lbServiceItems_DoubleClick( _
                  ByVal sender As System.Object, _
                  ByVal e As System.EventArgs) _
              Handles lbServiceItems.DoubleClick

  Dim localService As New ServiceController( _
            DirectCast(nameHolder(lbServiceItems.SelectedIndex), _
            Names).serviceName)

  Dim sb As New StringBuilder()
  Dim i As Integer

  'show service name
  sb.Append("Service Type: ")
  sb.Append(localService.ServiceType.ToString())
  sb.Append(Environment.NewLine)

  'show service name
  sb.Append("Dependency List: ")
```

```
'loop through the dependent services list
For i = 0 To localService.DependentServices.Length - 1
  sb.Append(localService.DependentServices(i).DisplayName)
  sb.Append(Environment.NewLine)
Next

'show the new form
Dim supp As New SupplementaryInfo()
supp.txtServiceInfo.Text = sb.ToString()
supp.Show()
End Sub
```

In the new form the `ServiceType` is shown, which will correlate to the service types illustrated in Chapter 2. From the service list (as opposed to the device list) most services will return `Win32OwnProcess` or `Win32ShareProcess`; however, a few may be marked as being an `InteractiveProcess` (this is set by a checkbox on the service property pages which allows the service to interact with the desktop).

The `DependentServices` property returns an array of `ServiceController` objects, so the display name is extracted and appended to our `Stringbuilder` object.

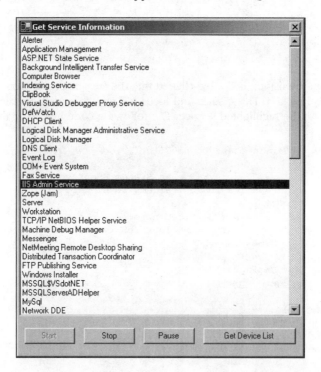

We shall revisit another way of writing this application later in the chapter when we examine the use of WMI. One point worth making before we move on to the next section is the flexibility we have the .NET classes. The `ServiceController` can be used to inspect the Windows Services running locally or remotely (a constructor overload takes a machine name parameter). The only consideration with using the application to connect to an SCM on a remote machine is the use of security, the credentials under which the logged on user is using the applications must either match similar credentials on the remote machine or they must be domain credentials that have enough permission to inspect the remote services. In a similar manner the MMC can be used in the same way. The Computer Management MMC application lists all the Microsoft snap-ins on the local machine but assuming the logged on user has appropriate authorization they can use the **Connect to another computer** option, which will enable them to control services remotely. This means that we can use a standard MMC interface for remote management of services.

Configuring Services

So we've seen how a service can be controlled through the basic mechanisms of the SCM. Let's look now at how exactly we can make the behavior of our service vary from machine to machine, or time to time, so that it can be applied to more varied and interesting tasks. There are essentially three points when we might want to configure a service:

❑ At install time: when the service is first installed, we might specify some settings that will apply every time it is run. Some settings are standard for all services, and we'll look at these shortly.

❑ At startup time: each time the service is run, we might want it to load some configuration settings from somewhere.

❑ At run time: while the service is running, we may need to change its mode of operation, or activate or deactivate functionality.

How can we accomplish each of these in the case of Windows Services?

Well, an installer can choose which components to install, can create configuration files, and can set up initial configuration of the service so that it will behave in a particular, customized way.

We can pass startup parameters to a service (we'll see how soon), or a service can load in parameters from a particular location on startup.

We can pass commands to a running service, or a service can expose controls via .NET remoting, WMI, or some other mechanism with common access between configuration tools and the service itself.

In reality, it may be possible to use a combined approach to all three. We can use installer classes to configure the service so that little in the way of later manual configuration is needed. In reality, most applications simply gather information at install time from the administrator, and use it to create a set of startup parameters for the service. This can be done in a variety of ways. Some applications use an .ini file and read in values and set global variables with these defined parameters. Registry keys can also be used to store similar values. More modern applications may use an XML file, or perhaps a database table. While it may seem necessary to use a GUI to provide continual run-time configuration, you could consider using a configuration file of this type. In .NET the `FileSystemWatcher`, a class of the `System.IO` namespace, can be used to monitor configuration file changes or directory changes, which can prompt services to change their configuration parameters "on the fly", when the configuration file's contents change. So, the use of such configuration information may be enough to provide support for all three configuration modes.

A common way to apply start up parameters is through the registry. In particular, this allows a service to store information when it is stopped, then collect that information again the next time it is started, providing a seamless service.

It's possible to pass startup parameters to a service directly every time the service starts. The parameters to pass can be set in the property pages for the service, the only caveat being that each time the service is stopped and restarted the interactive user must rewrite the startup parameters into the property pages textbox. The `Start()` method of the `ServiceController` class has an overload that takes a `String` array containing the startup parameters for the service. It is very easy to forget to apply the startup parameters so if this is your chosen means of initial service configuration for completeness it should be combined with a registry read operation that will act as the default if the specified service startup parameters are not present. When the property pages are closed the startup parameters for the service will disappear from the textbox window. Obviously, if your service is to be started and stopped via a GUI or web page, using the programmatic interface to the SCM, you can ensure that parameters are passed in from your code.

Install-Time Configuration

We can initially configure the name of service (the reference that the SCM and the `ServiceController` class will use to identify the service) at installation time as well as the account under which the service runs, the startup type, which can be `Manual`, `Automatic`, or `Disabled` (these are enumeration members), the display name of the service, and a string array containing all the services on which this service depends. Here's some code from a typical service that configures its installation parameters:

```
Me.ServiceInstaller1.ServiceName = "XMLData"
Me.ServiceInstaller1.StartType =
ServiceProcess.ServiceStartMode.Automatic
Me.ServiceInstaller1.DisplayName = "Xml Data Extraction Service"
Me.ServiceInstaller1.ServicesDependedOn() = New String() _
    {"MSSQLSERVER"}
```

These are the current limits to configuring the service programmatically using the .NET
ServiceInstaller class; however, custom actions can be written directly to the
registry for our own services (be careful, though: using this technique in the wrong
manner is certain to corrupt the application and possibly the operating system's vital
organs!). The Description and other aspects of the service can be configured here. Do
read the documentation thoroughly before attempting to alter these values.

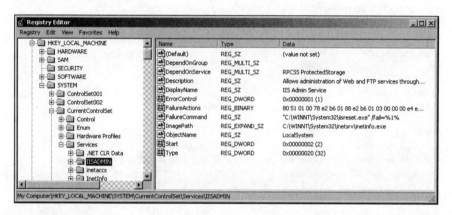

Building a Service with Command Interfaces

One interesting method exposed by the ServiceController class is the
ExecuteCommand method. This allows us to create a series of custom commands that a
client can use to perform an operation on the service. The client calls the
ExecuteCommand method, passing it an integer value between 128 and 255, and the
service handles the request by implementing the OnCustomCommand() method. All
values below 128 are system reserved values that contain the standard methods to control
and query services, such as stop, pause, and continue (but not start – that command is,
naturally, never sent to a running service). This is a way of extending the functionality of
the service to clients beyond that of the stop, start, pause, and continue controls.

This section will focus on adding command interfaces, and a couple of other
configuration systems, to the IISMon service we built in the last chapter.

We'll make it so that the service can have its e-mailing functionality turned on or off through a custom command. We'll also make it so that the e-mail address and SMTP server used, as well as the polling interval and the target server to watch, are configurable at startup. The service's initial configuration data is obtained through the startup parameter interface of the service property page as described earlier. If these startup parameters don't exist or if they don't conform to the application-specified parameter format (it's easy to forget to put these in when starting up a service) then the application will try to read various registry values which allow for its configuration using defaults, set at install time. If these methods fail, it will fall back on defaults.

Let's look at the changes. We're going to replace some of our constants with member variables. But we'll need new constants to store the names of the registry entries we're going to use. We'll also need to import the `Microsoft.Win32` namespace to provide registry support. The top of the `IISMon.vb` file now looks like this:

```
Imports System.ServiceProcess
Imports System.Web.Mail
Imports Microsoft.Win32

Public Class IISMon
    Inherits System.ServiceProcess.ServiceBase

    Private Const svcName As String = "W3SVC"
    Private Const regKey = "SOFTWARE\wrox\iismon"
    Private Const intervalKey As String = "pollInterval"
    Private Const machineKey As String = "targetMachine"
    Private Const emailKey As String = "emailAddress"
    Private Const smtpKey As String = "smtpServer"
    Private Const useMailKey As String = "useMail"

    Private monInterval As Integer = 300
    Private svcMachine As String = "."
    Private EmailTo As String = "administrator@localhost"
    Private smtpServer As String = "localhost"
    Private useEmail As Boolean = "True"

    Private cdTimer As System.Timers.Timer
    Private elEvents As New EventLog()
    Private SvcControl As ServiceController
    Private NoticeSent As Boolean = False
    Private PeriodsDown As Long
```

The `OnStart()` method now needs to begin by populating these variables with arguments.

```
Protected Overrides Sub OnStart(ByVal args() As String)

    ' Extract the correct values for the configurable
    ' status of the service
    If args.Length = 2 Then
        ' Try to use args, but assume they don't want mail
```

```
    Try
      monInterval = Convert.ToInt32(args(0))
      svcMachine = args(1)
      useEmail = False
    Catch e As Exception
    End Try
  ElseIf args.Length = 4 Then
    ' Try to use args, and assume they DO want mail
    Try
      monInterval = Convert.ToInt32(args(0))
      svcMachine = args(1)
      EmailTo = args(2)
      smtpServer = args(3)
      useEmail = True
    Catch e As Exception
    End Try
  Else
    'Check registry keys
    Try
      Dim reg As RegistryKey = _
          Registry.LocalMachine.OpenSubKey(regKey)
      monInterval = Convert.ToInt32(reg.GetValue(intervalKey))
      svcMachine = Convert.ToString(reg.GetValue(machineKey))
      EmailTo = Convert.ToString(reg.GetValue(emailKey))
      smtpServer = Convert.ToString(reg.GetValue(smtpKey))
      useEmail = Convert.ToBoolean(reg.GetValue(useMailKey))
    Catch e As Exception
    End Try
  End If

  ' Create a timer object with specified interval
  cdTimer = New Timers.Timer(Me.monInterval * 1000)
  ' Add an event handler for our new timer.
  AddHandler cdTimer.Elapsed, AddressOf Me.OnTimerElapsed
  cdTimer.Start()
  elEvents.Source = "IISMon"
  elEvents.WriteEntry("IIS Monitor starting with an interval of " _
      & Me.monInterval.ToString() & " seconds.", _
      EventLogEntryType.Information)
End Sub
```

In this example the parameters that are used are:

❑   The **monitoring interval**, which specifies how often the service will
   be polled

❑   The **target machine**, which specifies on which computer the service
   process will be monitored

❑   The **e-mail address** to mail if the server goes down

❑   The **SMTP server** to use for sending mail

If you specify two parameters, the service assumes they are the first two, and doesn't configure mail. If you specify all four, it assumes you want mail configured.

We also need to make one small change to the `OnTimerElapsed()` handler as well, to take account of the possibility that mail may not be set up:

```
If NoticeSent = True Then
   elEvents.Source = "IISMon"
   elEvents.WriteEntry("IIS is currently running", _
   EventLogEntryType.Information)

   If useEmail Then
      SendEmail("IIS is currently running on server " & svcMachine)
   End If
   ' Clear our flag.
   NoticeSent = False
End If
```

So, our service is a little bit more flexible. Now let's add the ability to change its behavior while it's running. The list of commands in this example service has been kept to a minimum just to illustrate their use; however, they can be as complicated and as numerous as necessary for the service. In our case, we'll have two:

❑   `SuppressMail`, which tells the service to stop sending out mails

❑   `UseMail`, which tells the service to make sure it sends out mails

We need to allocate each command a unique number between 128 and 255. We'll use 128 and 129. To make sure we never get confused about which command is which, we'll set up an enumeration, as follows:

```
Public Enum Commands
   SuppressMail = 128
   UseMail = 129
End Enum
```

To handle these commands, the `OnCustomCommand()` method of the `ServiceBase` class must be overridden in our service class. The command takes the form of an integer which can be converted into a task by using `If ... Then ... Else` or `Select ... Case` blocks to select an activity based on the command value.

```
Protected Overrides Sub OnCustomCommand(ByVal command As Int32)
   Select Case command
      Case Commands.SuppressMail
         useEmail = False
      Case Commands.UseMail
         useEmail = True
   End Select
End Sub
```

Earlier in the chapter we discussed how we would execute a command from the client. The client will obtain a handle to the service using the `ServiceController` class and call the `ExecuteCommand()` method. The `ExecuteCommand()` method will allow an integer value to be passed to the service. The service will then invoke the `OnCustomCommand()` method, which will handle the command value. For example, the following code would obtain a handle to the IISAdmin service and execute a command that would result in the service suppressing future e-mails.

```
Dim svc As New ServiceController("IISAdmin")
svc.ExecuteCommand(IISAdmin.Commands.SuppressMail)
```

Building a GUI Controller

A thoroughly important aspect of client development is the GUI that we choose. Services lend themselves well to certain types of GUI to allow a user to control their behavior. The type of GUI used could depend on many aspects such as the client runtime, the simplicity, whether the control is to be interactive, whether the service is one of many of the same type of service located throughout a network, security constraints, and firewall constraints.

In this section, we'll look at two common graphical interfaces used to control a service while it's running. We'll see how to attach a system tray icon to a service, and how to build an MMC snap-in.

There is one other common solution, which as yet we cannot put into place using VB.NET; this is a control panel applet. This could be developed in C++ using unmanaged code. There is no reason why any of the mechanisms described above could not be incorporated into a client applet written in C++ to control a service. This, however, is beyond the scope of this book.

Using the System Tray

The use of a **system tray** icon to show status and provide a control mechanism for a service is commonplace. In order to create a system tray icon for a service we must create a Windows form. But as we know, we can't have interactive UI components running in the Windows Service space. It is possible to create non-interactive systray icons, to report on service status, from within the service. But an interactive systray icon will have to run as a user process.

We can create a simple system tray controller program, by creating a Windows forms application with a single main form that is invisible to the user – to accomplish this, we make the form's `ShowInTaskbar` property `False`, and its `WindowState` property `Minimized`.

A system tray icon is represented in .NET by a `NotifyIcon` component, which you'll find in the Windows forms toolbox in VS. To create a simple system-tray icon project, create a new Windows Forms project, and add a `NotifyIcon` to its main form. Set the forms properties to make it invisible, as we said – minimized, but invisible in the taskbar. To enable us to interact with the application we need to allow the user to bring up a menu, so we must add a `ContextMenu` to the form, and set the `NotifyIcon`'s `ContextMenu` property to that `ContextMenu`. Then you can add items to the context menu, and `Click` event handlers to the context items. Don't forget to include one option to stop the system tray application, since without an active form with a close button, there's no clean way to stop such a program. We can also trap 'click' and 'double-click' events on the icon itself.

The image the icon uses is set using its `Icon` property, which you can set to the icon from an `.ico` file using the VS.NET properties window. You can manipulate the icon programmatically using GDI+, as well as just loading the image from a file.

Developing an MMC Snap-In

By far the most familiar GUI for a service is an MMC snap-in. The MMC provides us with the opportunity to manage our Windows Service using a standard interface, which can be customized to display not just our service application but other MMC snap-ins. For example, the admin interface for XDE could be configured to show the SQL Server snap-in as well.

Unfortunately the MMC is COM-based, and doesn't know how to run managed code, which makes development of MMC snap-ins in .NET rather difficult. There are, however, actually several ways to develop a snap-in in .NET.

❑ Create a C# class with a COM interface (using the `ComImport` attribute to publish the .NET classes as COM classes). This approach, actually demonstrated in an early Microsoft example, is frowned upon by the MMC team (the C# project used to illustrate this was removed from the .NET team site, http://www.gotdotnet.com, prior to the release of Beta 2 of the Framework). It is also virtually impossible to synthesize in VB.NET as it involves the use of non-CLR types. You could code the skeleton of such a class in C#, and extend it in VB.NET (or any other .NET language).

❑ Use the Visual C++ ATL wizard.

❑ Extend an MMC application by using XML to extend the view (this is covered in the MSDN Magazine article cited earlier in the chapter). This approach is only available to MMC 2.0 on Windows XP. It doesn't precisely allow us to create a snap-in, but allows us to customize the snap-in view.

❑ Use the VB designer provided by the Platform SDK to write the snap-in in VB6, but write the functional part of the snap-in that controls our service using VB.NET.

The most obvious implementation for VB developers is the last one (although it does require us to have access to an installation of Visual Basic 6). In order to create an MMC snap-in we must use the VB MMC Snap-In Designer provided with the core Microsoft Platform SDK (the Platform SDK is generally updated every three months and is available for download from the MSDN web site).

To develop our partially .NET MMC snap-in, for a .NET Windows service called XMLData, we'll need to build a COM component in VB.NET that can be accessed by the VB6 snap-in we'll be creating. A VB.NET project called XmlServiceStatus is used to contain all the code that will control the actual service. We begin by declaring a member variable to contain an XDE service ServiceController object.

```
Imports System.Diagnostics
Imports System.ServiceProcess
Imports System.Runtime.InteropServices

Public Class XmlServiceStatus

   Private svc As New ServiceController("XMLData")
```

Our COM component will present one read-only property, which client code will use to query the status of the service, and several methods, which, when called, issue a command to the service. This will enable our VB6 snap-in to communicate, via our .NET code, with the service itself.

For the property that returns the status of the XDE service, we simply return an integer value. Notice the use of the ComVisible attribute. This will ensure that this class property will be visible to COM irrespective of the scope declaration.

```
   <System.Runtime.InteropServices.ComVisible(True)> _
   Public ReadOnly Property Status() As Integer
     Get
       If svc.Status = (ServiceControllerStatus.Running _
                    Or ServiceControllerStatus.StartPending) Then
         Status = 0
       End If
       If svc.Status = (ServiceControllerStatus.Stopped _
                    Or ServiceControllerStatus.StopPending) Then
         Status = 1
       End If
       If svc.Status = (ServiceControllerStatus.Paused _
                    Or ServiceControllerStatus.Paused) Then
         Status = 2
       End If
     End Get
   End Property
```

Similarly, six methods are present that perform similar operations to all the other clients we have developed.

```
  <System.Runtime.InteropServices.ComVisible(True)> _
  Public Sub StopXmlService()
    svc.Stop()
  End Sub

  <System.Runtime.InteropServices.ComVisible(True)> _
  Public Sub StartXmlService()
    svc.Start()
  End Sub

  <System.Runtime.InteropServices.ComVisible(True)> _
  Public Sub PauseXmlService()
    svc.Pause()
  End Sub

  <System.Runtime.InteropServices.ComVisible(True)> _
  Public Sub ResumeXmlService()
    svc.Continue()
  End Sub

  <System.Runtime.InteropServices.ComVisible(True)> _
  Public Sub TimerStopXmlService()
    svc.ExecuteCommand(130)
  End Sub

  <System.Runtime.InteropServices.ComVisible(True)> _
  Public Sub TimerStartXmlService()
    svc.ExecuteCommand(131)
  End Sub
End Class
```

The most important aspect though, is that we use the project property pages to register the COM output and generate a COM proxy.

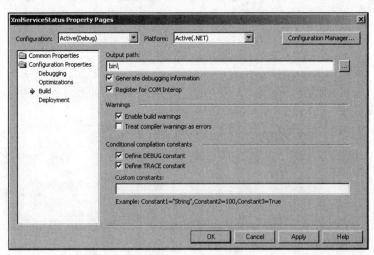

After creating and registering a COM interop project from VB.NET we can begin to create the MMC snap-in in VB6. As we said before, the snap-in designer is included in the Microsoft Platform SDK. The relevant snap-in files need to be copied to the VB template projects directory and we have to register three DLL and OCX controls. It must be remembered that if this snap-in is distributed to clients then these three DLL/OCX files must be distributed too.

Here are the exact steps required:

- ❑ Copy all the files from the platform SDK's `Samples\SysMgmt\mmc\Visual Basic\Template` directory to Visual Basic 6's `Templates\Projects` directory

- ❑ Register the following three libraries in the Platform SDK's `bin` directory using the system `regsvr32.exe` program:

  - `mmcproxy.dll`

  - `mssnapd.ocx`

  - `mssnapr.dll`

Now, when you start up VB6, you'll be presented with a new project option, SnapIn:

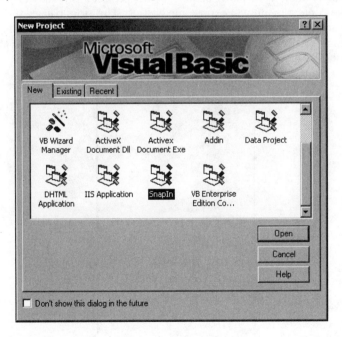

A snap-in project will contain a single snap-in object, which will present the following unusual looking interface when double-clicked:

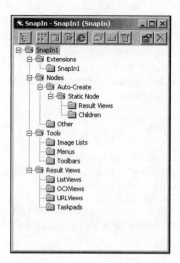

This allows us to access each aspect of our MMC snap-in, configure its properties, and add elements such as property pages and menus to the program.

We will keep the VB snap-in simple using a single context menu on the root node (called the static node) of the MMC snap-in (in our project this node will have no children). The context menu will expose methods to start, stop, pause, and resume the XDE service and to start and stop a timer. Each menu must be added to the designer by right-clicking on the Tools | Menus designer node and choosing the Add Menu option. Here's what the designer looks like for our XmlSnapIn project:

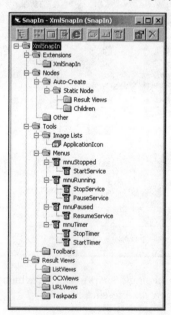

As you can see, the menu choices must be hierarchical to function correctly. A parent menu must be specified and a child menu added to that, when the parent menu is made visible at run time within the code all child menu items will be added to the context menu. There is a great deal that we can do with the MMC. We have a scope, results, and view pane, which we can utilize to offer virtually any type of management functionality but we will only be focusing on the view pane and specifically a context menu that will execute commands through the VB.NET assembly via COM interop. An MMC snap-in guide for VB exists in the Platform SDK documentation that details the complete functionality and programming techniques for the designer.

Now we can bring up the code view. Before beginning to add event handlers to the snap-in, we must first add a reference to our VB.NET COM DLL XmlServiceStatus. As this has been registered with a COM typelib we can simply add it from the Project | References menu where it will be visible. Following this, in the VB code designer view we can declare a member variable of type XmlServiceStatus.

```
Dim service As New XmlServiceStatus.XmlServiceStatus
```

Each of the child menu items can have its own event handler, which can be created by double-clicking on the menu item in the designer view. The result is shown below, so in effect all we must do is add some implementation code. We simply call our .NET code through our COM DLL.

```
Private Sub StartTimer_Click(ByVal Index As Long, _
   ByVal Selection As SnapInLib.MMCClipboard), _
      service.StartTimerXmlService
End Sub
```

We can use the Views_AddNewMenuItems() method to add the menu items to the context menu at run time. This is called when the XmlSnapIn static node is right-clicked in the MMC view pane. One of the parameters passed into this method (ContextMenu) represents the actual menu that is being built. We add items to it by calling the AddMenu() method to add each parent menu to the context menu. This method will test for the relevant status through the VB.NET DLL property: XmlServiceStatus.

```
Private Sub Views_AddNewMenuItems(ByVal View As SnapInLib.View, _
               ByVal Selection As SnapInLib.MMCClipboard, _
               ByVal ContextMenu As SnapInLib.ContextMenu, _
               InsertionAllowed As Boolean)
   If service.Status = 0 Then
      ContextMenu.AddMenu mnuStopped
   ElseIf service.Status = 1 Then
      ContextMenu.AddMenu mnuRunning
   ElseIf service.Status = 2 Then
      ContextMenu.AddMenu mnuPaused
   End If
   ContextMenu.AddMenu mnuTimer
End Sub
```

The resulting snap-in is actually an ActiveX Control (an OCX). Most snap-ins are DLL files but the MMC is indifferent to the file output type. We can test the snap-in in real time by simply debugging the project; we can also debug across development environments from VB to VB.NET. In order to use the snap-in, however, we have to set a registry entry for it. To do this we need to do a quick registry search for the GUID that VB has assigned to the compiled COM control `SnapIn.ocx`. When this is done we can build a `.reg` file to register the component with the MMC. To register the XDE snap-in with MMC we would use:

```
REGEDIT4

[HKEY_LOCAL_MACHINE\Software\Microsoft\MMC\Snapins\{83A20487-62DF-
4CE7-93E6-E18B2AC365A0}]
"NameString" = "Xml Snap In"

[HKEY_LOCAL_MACHINE\Software\Microsoft\MMC\Snapins\{83A20487-62DF-
4CE7-93E6-E18B2AC365A0}\StandAlone]
```

> *Before compiling the `SnapIn.vbp` project we should ensure that binary compatibility is turned on in the project properties.*

Run this `.reg` file by double-clicking it, and your snap-in is registered. Obviously, you can build installer programs that can handle this process more cleanly for an end user.

Once the snap-in has been registered we can start the MMC by typing mmc at the run prompt or on a command line (or even in the address bar of explorer). Once it has loaded we simply choose the Add/Remove Snap-in... option from the Console menu, and browse to the XmlSnapIn.

Using the MMC to develop snap-ins is relatively easy with VB and the designer project. Coupling this with COM interop and the power of .NET we can achieve spectacular management results for our service. A further step would be to use the designer to create child nodes for XDE services on remote machines.

The uses and possibilities for the MMC are numerous. It enables us to have an elegant, flexible, and familiar management solution for any possible service we could think of writing.

Control Through WMI

WMI (Windows Management Instrumentation) is the Microsoft implementation of the WBEM (Web-Based Enterprise Management) standard. It provides a framework for the management of applications using OO principles. WMI allows control of much of the operating system having representative WMI classes for virtually all type of device, operating system, and Windows Services. WMI support is also built into applications such as SQL Server, which allows the inspection and control of the underlying SQL Server databases using standard WMI interfaces. Each WMI base class is registered with the **Management schema** and each class instance is registered with the **Management catalog** (a database of all instances of WMI classes). WMI enables us to do several things:

❑   It allows us to convert our `Data` class into a WMI class so that the `GetXml` method can be called and information on the service can be retrieved by inspecting its instance variables

❑   It allows us to rewrite the original `AllServices` application to use a WMI consumer instead of the `ServiceController` class, demonstrating WMI control of Windows Services

The **AllServicesWMI** application will use WMI instead of the `ServiceController` class to retrieve the list of application services (not the list of device driver services – as these involve other WMI classes) and issue standard start, stop, pause, and continue commands to the selected service.

There are two ways to consume WMI classes from our applications, and we'll be using both.

The first is to use the built-in support of the .NET Framework for management base classes. Our code interacts with generic management classes, and requests methods and properties that it wishes to access by specifying their name as a string. This requires our code to know what each class can do and what its methods and properties are. We can inspect each WMI class at run time to reveal all the properties and methods that it supports on its WMI interface, but this method is still error-prone, though it has its applications for dealing with generic management tasks.

The second provides "early binding" support to allow us to create classes that we can compile our code against, so that our .NET application has access to specified methods and properties, which appear on a .NET object, which will abstract the underlying WMI instance. This enables us to use IntelliSense in Visual Studio, and we get the compiler's help in checking that we only access methods and properties that are appropriate for a particular instance.

The WMI class that represents an abstract base class for all Windows Services is called `Win32_Service`. Similarly, other abstract base classes exist, which can be used to provide generic information on printers, networking cards, etc. In order to create a .NET proxy class for the `Win32_Service` class to allow our application to encapsulate instances of the WMI class `Win32_Service` with a .NET object, we can use the `mgmtclassgen.exe` utility (this utility can be used from the VS.NET command prompt). Using the `/L` switch we can generate the output proxy class file in a variety of languages. This command will produce a VB.NET output file called `service.vb`, which defines a class called `Service` in the `ROOT.CIMV2.Win32` namespace:

```
> mgmtclassgen /L VB Win32_Service
```

The default namespace for this class actually matches the WMI namespace of the class (`ROOT.CIMV2`). This namespace is the default for almost all the system WMI classes. `Win32` is a subset of this namespace used only to group all Win32 WMI classes together. You can just add this source file to a project to make the class available to your code. If you're building a lot of WMI applications that use the same WMI classes, you could create a DLL of these generated management classes and reference it from all the projects that use them.

In our code we will use both the early-bound proxy class, and late-bound dynamic control of the WMI class directly, to illustrate the techniques involved in each type of use.

Let's look at the changes to `Services.vb` that are required to use WMI instead of `ServiceProcess`.

In order to turn our application into a WMI consumer we must set a reference to the `System.Management.dll` assembly and import the namespace.

```
Imports System
Imports System.ServiceProcess
Imports System.Collections
Imports System.Text
Imports System.Management
```

The event handler for the Get Service List button wants to obtain a WMI instance for each of the Windows Services on the system. It does so using a query, which it passes to a ManagementObjectSearcher object. This returns a set of WMI objects that match the search criteria. In our case, the criterion is simply 'give me all the objects that are Windows Services'. We express the query in a language called WQL (WMI Query Language). A thorough description of WQL is beyond the scope of the chapter but it is similar in construction to SQL, such that properties of WMI classes can be obtained and WMI classes and events queried using a SQL-like syntax. More information on WQL can be found at http://msdn.microsoft.com/library/en-us/wmisdk/wmi/querying_with_wql.asp, which also covers subscriptions to WMI event notifications. Our use of WQL here is very rudimentary and searches simply for objects of the specified class: Win32_Service. All instances of the Win32_Service class registered with the Management catalog will be returned.

Here are the changes we need to make to the actual btGetServices event handler:

```
Private Sub btGetServices_Click(ByVal sender As System.Object, _
                        ByVal e As System.EventArgs) _
            Handles btGetServices.Click

    Dim scm As ServiceController()
    Dim i As Integer = 0
    Dim isServices As Boolean = True

    nameHolder.Clear()
    lbServiceItems.Items.Clear()
    If Not m_Services Then
        isServices = False
        m_Services = True
    Else
        m_Services = False
    End If

    If isServices Then
        Dim selectQuery As New SelectQuery("Win32_Service")
        Dim mgrObjectSearcher As New ManagementObjectSearcher(selectQuery)
```

This is where we set up the query. The ManagementObjectSearcher is configured with a WQL query, but won't execute it until we call Get(). When we do call this method, we'll receive a ManagementObjectCollection (which is a collection of ManagementObjects). We simply enumerate the members of the collection using a For ... Each loop and create a new instance of the generated ROOT.CIMV2.Win32.Service class using the ManagementObject (currentManagementObject) as the constructor parameter.

```
Dim currentManagementObject As ManagementObject
For Each currentManagementObject In mgrObjectSearcher.Get()
  Dim scmServer As New _
      ROOT.CIMV2.Win32.Service(currentManagementObject)
  lbServiceItems.Items.Add(scmServer.DisplayName)
  Dim n As Names
  n.displayName = scmServer.DisplayName
  n.serviceName = scmServer.Name
  nameHolder.Add(n)
Next
```

Using the proxy class enables us to make method and property calls directly. Examples of this in the code above are to retrieve the `DisplayName` and `Name` properties (which relate to the display name and the short name of the service). The code adds the display name to the `Names` structure and to the listbox as it did before using the `ServiceController` class.

We handle device lookups using the same logic as before.

```
Else
  scm = currentService.GetDevices()
  While (i < scm.Length - 1)
    lbServiceItems.Items.Add(scm(i).DisplayName)
    Dim n As Names
    n.displayName = scm(i).DisplayName
    n.serviceName = scm(i).ServiceName
    nameHolder.Add(n)
    i = i + 1
  End While
End If

  butGetServices.Text = "Get Services List"
  If isServices Then butGetServices.Text = "Get Device List"
End Sub
```

The next block of code will just show how we can use the WMI class directly through the `ManagementObject` class rather than through the proxy to start the service. The stop, pause, and continue functions are not reproduced here but are written in the same manner.

Since we know the name of the service we wish to control (the user has selected the listbox item as in the `AllServices` application), we can use a more precise form of query to obtain the precise management object we want. Specifically, we can use the `ManagementPath` class to define the path to the `Win32_Service` we want. By using `Win32_Service.Name` and specifying the name of the service we can restrict the return value to one management object. A `ManagementPath` is an absolute path, which must return one WMI class instance – unlike a query, which may return many, or none at all. When the `Get()` method is called, the object is retrieved.

Now, we have an instance of ManagementObject. We need to call methods specific to a service, however, to start, stop, or pause it. The InvokeMethod() method on the ManagementObject can be used to invoke a method on the corresponding WMI Win32_Service instance. The names of the methods differ slightly from the methods of the same function on the ServiceController class. They are.

❑   StartService

❑   StopService

❑   PauseService

❑   ResumeService

Let's look at the logic for starting a service:

```
Private Sub btStart_Click(ByVal sender As System.Object, _
                          ByVal e As System.EventArgs) _
                Handles btStart.Click
    Dim localService As New ManagementObject( _
                    New ManagementPath("Win32_Service.Name='" + _
                DirectCast(nameHolder(lbServiceItems.SelectedIndex), _
                            Names).serviceName + _
                                    "'"))
    localService.Get()
    If CheckHighlighted() Then
      Try
        localService.InvokeMethod("StartService", Nothing)
      Catch ex As Exception
        MessageBox.Show(ex.Message)
      End Try
    End If
End Sub
```

Property values can be retrieved from a WMI class instance, as well. The following code is taken from the SelectedItemChanged event handler of the listbox control. Property values can be retrieved by using an indexer on the ManagementObject. This will return a property value of type Object, so it must be cast using CType or DirectCast. The State property on the WMI class is equivalent to the Status property on the ServiceController class. This property will return a String value, which will be one of:

❑   STOPPED

❑   RUNNING

❑   PAUSED

Unlike with the ServiceControllerStatus enumeration, we must do string comparison to check the state of the service.

```
If CType(localService("State"), String).ToUpper() = "STOPPED" Then
   btStop.Enabled = False
Else
   btStop.Enabled = True
End If
If CType(localService("State"), String).ToUpper() = "RUNNING" Then
   btStart.Enabled = False
Else
   btStart.Enabled = True
End If
   btPause.Enabled = True
If CType(localService("State"), String).ToUpper() = "PAUSED" Then
   btPause.Text = "Continue"
Else
   btPause.Text = "Pause"
End If
```

WMI is a powerful tool for controlling and querying the status of a computer system programmatically. It's also possible for us to publish our own WMI classes and create advanced control mechanisms that are open to any WMI client.

Summary

This chapter has focused on the way that we configure and control Windows Services. We have shown that services can be controlled through mechanisms in .NET, through fundamental Windows technologies. We have also discussed how to configure Windows Services such that they can be parameterized in a variety of ways to allow for greater flexibility. The mechanisms of control are numerous, as has been demonstrated, and the flexibility with which we can develop a UI for the service allows for a great deal of choice in how we develop an interactive control mechanism for the service.

In this chapter we covered:

- ❑ Basic control of services

- ❑ Using command-line utilities and property pages to configure services

- ❑ Using the `ServiceController` class

- ❑ Executing custom commands

- ❑ Developing a system tray GUI

- ❑ Creating an MMC snap-in for multiple services

- ❑ Service management using WMI

In the next chapter, we'll move on to look at how services can look outwards, onto a network, to get control and configuration data, or to provide their services to other remote machines – and see how deploying services in a networked environment raises development and deployment issues we've not encountered so far with our local services.

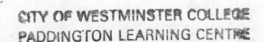

VB.NET

Windows Services

Handbook

5

5

Network-Oriented Services

Now that we have built and configured a Windows Service that runs locally, it is time to look at how to build, execute, and work with a Windows Service placed on a remote machine. Remote services take many different forms from initiating processes such as SQL Server, IIS, and working with these, through to services that are constantly used from computer boot through to shutdown, such as print spooler and plug-and-play. A local service does offer the developer and user some control over its execution and execution state but when you have a service on a remote computer you do have to rely on certain conditions being met to effectively install and run it. We will look at this before we create and deploy our examples.

Interaction with a remote service also brings its own problems. You are now no longer keeping the process within the realms of your own piece of hardware but there are now networks, remote machines, security, and interacting with that service over a domain, all to be considered. There are different methods of achieving the goal of working with remote Windows Services and we will look at two of these in this chapter: TCP/IP connections and Microsoft Message Queue – MSMQ. Both of these methods need to marshal requests.

We will also look at how to incorporate message queuing into a Windows Service when there is a need to ensure that messages sent to a service are processed in a timely manner.

By the end of this chapter you will:

- ❑ Build a Windows Service working with TCP/IP
- ❑ See how to debug a service remotely

- ❏ Be working with threads and listeners
- ❏ See remote installations
- ❏ Have experienced MSMQ processing of actions

Communicating with Remote Services

When you have built your Windows Service and installed it on a remote machine, you are presented with several problems. One of the first ones you will have to deal with concerns dealing with the information that the service has contained within it or has to retrieve. Both of the examples demonstrated in this chapter, just like most services you build, will have information that you want to be able to retrieve and work with.

If the service is on a local computer, when building a Visual Basic .NET program, all that is required is a reference to the service DLL. An instance of that object within your VB.NET program will allow you to utilize calls just as you would with any other DLL.

When you are working with objects in a local DLL, all that happens once it is referenced is that the compiler knows where the code for the necessary classes is contained. It knows where the constructor and any static/shared members can be found. When a new object is created, it can allocate memory from the managed heap to contain all the required code and store a reference to it in the area of memory reserved for the `ServiceBase`-derived object.

This is simple when working with a local DLL call, but what are your options when working with a remote object? You could write a text file, XML file, or some other similar object to the remote computer for it to read by simply using a UNC path to the server and the drive.

> *UNC, or Universal Naming Convention, is one way of referencing a server, for example* `\\remoteserver01\sharename`.

Another possible method of working with a remote object would be to use a database to which both computers could create a connection. Neither of these options is very practical from a Windows Service viewpoint.

So what better solutions are there? Well there are two excellent methods of working with remote objects and Windows Services and these involve **TCP/IP**, and **MSMQ** to pass messages. The third method revolves around Remoting, and this is covered in great detail in the *Visual Basic .NET Remoting Handbook* (ISBN: 1-86100-740-X).

It is also possible to use the inbuilt OnCustomCommand() *method of a service for communication, but you are then reliant on the client computer having full access rights to the server's services, which on a network server would be undesirable due to the security implications.*

There are two example applications within this chapter each using one of the methods mentioned above. The first example service watches the event log on a remote computer and when an error arrives, it broadcasts a notification to any clients listening in.

The second example makes use of a message queue for a system that deals with pricing and trading in shares. In this instance we will build a DLL, because as a Windows Service, we need to incorporate the MSMQ reference that will ensure that price quotations and orders are completed in a safe and secure manner. The network communication in this case takes place with the MSMQ service.

We will first look at TCP/IP.

TCP/IP

When communicating over an intranet or the Internet, as a Windows Service might do, it is important to understand how TCP/IP works. We will briefly describe TCP/IP first, and relate this to the Window Service we'll be creating.

TCP/IP is an error-correcting, "**connectionless**" method (meaning a server need know nothing of the client connecting, other than its address) of connecting computers and networks together, and therefore creating a network communication link between them. One large, Windows Service-based, application using this method is Symantec's *pcAnywhere*, where a TCP/IP connection is made either through the company intranet or over the Internet between two computers and allowing the client computer to view and control the host computer. The TCP/IP link in this instance sends commands from a client computer to the remote computer via a link in the client's remote access process to one on the remote computer. pcAnywhere on the remote computer is initially started up through a Windows Service and this service, through DLLs on the remote computer, sets up a TCP/IP connection to listen and broadcast information.

When you work on a computer that is part of a TCP/IP, from a command prompt it is possible to find out the computer's IP address and subnet mask by entering **ipconfig**. This details a unique TCP/IP address for your computer, which will be unique within the domain of the network. A domain could be unique within one location, for example the Wrox office in Birmingham, or if it talks directly to the Internet, then it will be unique across the world. Addresses that start with 10. and 192.168. are reserved for use in private networks, like the Birmingham Wrox office, and machines on that network do not have a direct connection to the Internet, but connect through a proxy service or NAT (Network Address Translation) firewall. It would be possible to set up a computer in Birmingham and another in the Chicago sales office with the same private TCP/IP address.

While this would be a valid scenario if the two offices were not directly connected over a **Wide Area Network**, or **VPN**, as the two offices are connected, there would be conflicts and the two computers would no longer be able to communicate with the rest of the network, or each other. Therefore, a TCP/IP address needs to be unique. Although an address is a string representation of a 4-byte number, there is also a friendly DNS name, which resolves into this IP address. This is very similar to web addresses. The Wrox web site has an IP address of 204.148.170.161, but everyone knows it as www.wrox.com. It is the same in an organization. Just as the TCP/IP of the computer address has to be unique, so does the name of the computer. As both the address and the name are unique, this gives us two methods whenever we wish to connect to a computer, either by the address or by the name.

TCP/IP has been designed for unreliable networks. If any part of the data is lost or corrupted, then the data can be resent (on request from the client). If no acknowledgment is sent from a client that a packet has been received OK, then the server will send no more to that address until a new request is made. Protocols such as Multicasting provide a slight variation to this, but we needn't worry about such protocols here.

In the first example, we will be creating a TCP/IP connection between the server's Windows Service, which is monitoring an Event Log, and any client that wishes to connect.

When using TCP/IP as the method for communicating between two computers, it is not enough to simply have the IP address. TCP requires an additional port number. This is analogous to when a cellular phone transmitter is sending out hundreds of calls, like the server, and your cellular phone itself is only listening and working with one specific call, like the client. By prefixing the call with your cellular phone number, the port, then you know that you are working with the right process. Without ports, every service would require a separate IP address (something that is proposed with the IPv6 standard).

There may be many different services or processes wishing to communicate with other computers and there has to be a method of knowing that a listening process is working with the correct remote process.

Event Log Monitor

As we have mentioned, the first example we will be taking a look at is a service that will monitor the event log of a remote computer. The service will be running on the remote server checking its own local event log. This will be a configurable service and it will be possible to define which event log to monitor and which events it will be catching and detailing back to you. As you read in Chapter 3, three Windows event logs are present in all Windows computers, one for Application events, another for Security events, and one for System events. There may be other logs created by Windows Services, applications, or computer administrators for many other processes that a site may wish to separate, but it will be the standard three that we will be concentrating on here. We have hard-coded the example to monitor the Application Log, but you could easily alter this through an argument in the OnStart() method.

This example will be demonstrated dealing with application events as this will be the easiest to create but a more realistic example may be one that is monitoring for virus hits and reporting these back to a central point. Although the anti-virus software could deal with it, you may wish to be notified that you have had a hit so you know what is happening on your servers. Another possible use of this monitor would be to monitor a log of any potential security breaches or even any system problems that are being recorded, like hardware or driver failures. As you can see the scope for such an application is large.

We will start the service and build our event log monitoring but will not start monitoring until at least one client has connected. Once a client has connected we will wait from then until an event is created. After an event is found, a signal is then sent out to all clients informing them of such an event.

TCP/IP Listening and Broadcasting

To build a TCP listener it is crucial to know the sequence of events that occur from setting up the process listening for clients through what happens when a client sends a request and then dealing with subsequent messages.

To ensure that the host is ready for requests to connect, a process thread needs to be created and needs to be listening for any information being passed to it. This **thread** will listen for any information that comes to it once it has been started and will pass this on to a specific routine to check the contents and decide if it has come from a predefined **port** that we are listening to. The listener will then wait and eventually a client computer will pass through to the remote computer a connection via the necessary port. The thread hears this connection, knows that the port matches the port we desire, and we then have a TCPClient object within our system. In the example we are building, we take this TCPClient on the remote server, and store it as this provides the link between the two computers. Now we know we have an incoming link we set up a handling system for any messages delivered from the client and wait. So now we have an incoming connection a return code is sent back to the calling client computer to inform it that everything has been processed.

With the link established, the client computer will pass through a message to the remote computer asking to be set up to receive messages from the remote computer. As we have a message coming in to the remote computer the handler deals with it as is necessary and as we have a link established, we can respond to the message informing the client that the request has been processed. That is the process, so let's start building the example.

Figure 1

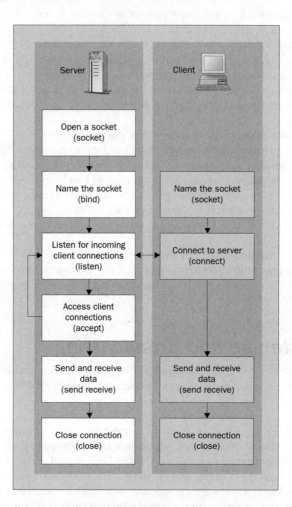

First of all we need to set up the TCP/IP listener and broadcasting capabilities of the service. This functionality is coded separately to the Windows Service class as it needs to be placed in a class library on its own, but still held within the Windows Service itself, so that we can create instances of the listener and broadcaster for each client that connects. Each instance created is placed into an `ArrayList`, so that when we wish to send messages out, all that is required is to iterate through the collection and broadcast the message needed.

As this class is going to be passing information between two computers, we need to implement a strategy to do this. The System.Net.Sockets namespace manages the marshaling of information to and from the client computer and the remote computer. By providing the ability to send and receive between two TCP/IP connections through a specific port number using sockets there is no need to specifically build code to marshal information over a network; all of this is done for you. However, in this case, both the client and the remote computer have to be listening on the same port once the connection is made. This then would allow several connections between the same two computers for different processes to listen for messages from the respective processes without getting the messages interwoven or having to build the need for decryption of messages to ensure that what was received was for that particular process and not another one. Although we are setting the socket connection at this point, it is not until the class is instantiated that we need to provide the port that we are going to use. More on this when we look at the Windows Service.

TCPListener

Create a new Visual Basic .NET Windows Service project and call it RemoteLogMon. In the Project Properties, set the Assembly name to RemoteLogMonitor. Add a new VB.NET class library and call it TCPBroadcast. Import the System.Net.Sockets namespace and also the System.Text namespace so we can work with text information that is being streamed into and out of our class instance. The following code implements the class we'll use for the TCPClient connection:

```
Imports System.Net.Sockets
Imports System.Text

Public Class TCPBroadcast
  Const READ_BUFFER_SIZE As Integer = 255
```

We now need to create a TCPClient that will provide us with the connection through WinSock to a remote computer. This object will then allow us the ability to pass and receive information that is passed through the Sockets connection we make when we start the Windows Service.

```
    Private client As TcpClient
    Private readBuffer(READ_BUFFER_SIZE) As Byte
    Private _name As String
```

When we create a new instance of this class every time a client computer connects, we will be passed in the TCP/IP listener that has received our request. Once we have the listener connection from the client, we can then begin an asynchronous read. By having the read asynchronous we are not stopping the thread of the Windows Service from running and this TCPClient will now wait until the connected client transmits.

109

An asynchronous read will act as soon as data is received rather than waiting until the whole data stream is sent. Therefore we need to have a handler enabled to deal with the stream of data and build it together as each byte is received. So although it appears as though it is reading the stream, this is not the case. All we have is a signal that is saying that there is data to read, so we need to pass control to a method to do this. When the signal that there is data to read is received and the sending of the data is complete we need to set up a callback to execute at this point. This is where the `StreamReceived()` method comes in to play, which we will explain in a moment.

```
Public Sub New(ByVal listener As TcpClient)
   Me.client = listener

   ' This starts the asynchronous read thread
   ' The data will be saved into readBuffer
   Me.client.GetStream.BeginRead(readBuffer, 0, _
                                 READ_BUFFER_SIZE, _
                                 AddressOf StreamReceived, _
                                 Nothing)
End Sub
```

It will be useful to uniquely identify this instance of the connection. The client can pass across any relevant information; in this case we will be passing the computer name.

```
Public Property Name() As String
   Get
      Return _name
   End Get

   Set(ByVal value As String)
      _name = value
   End Set
End Property
```

When the data arrives, we now have to deal with it. As you saw a few moments ago, we reach this method from a signal we received. By asking the `TCPClient` to give us the stream of data, we can then process it, but we could have hundreds of connections of which others may also be passing information. This would not cause a problem as we have individual instances of the client, but you could find that the client itself is transmitting information faster than the server is reading it. Each item of data is arriving on a specific **thread**, and if we have multiple threads running then the stream of data will become interwoven as a result. While the stream of data is coming in, we therefore stop any further threads executing on this stream by declaring a `SyncLock`. A `SyncLock` must operate on a reference type (anything that isn't a value type) and it prevents the code from executing on more than one thread at once. When this point in the code is reached during execution, then it will only execute the code in the loop when the object passed as an argument is not referenced by a currently executing `SyncLock` block.

```
Private Sub StreamReceived(ByVal asRes As IAsyncResult)
Dim BytesRead As Integer
Dim Message As String

Try
    SyncLock client.GetStream
        ' Once stream is read we need to know the bytes read
        ' So we can build in to a message
        BytesRead = client.GetStream.EndRead(asRes)
    End SyncLock
```

All the data is now read as we have had an end of stream notification processed, a Chr(13) and Chr(10). By taking the stream and removing that notification we now have the full message. We can then pass this on to a separate subroutine for processing. When we come across the DataReceived() method within the Windows Service, it is there that we will be processing the messages, such as the notification of the client's intent to listen or end listening. We then need to start up a new asynchronous read that will then respond when any new information is collected.

```
    ' Convert the message minus the terminator characters
    Message = Encoding.ASCII.GetString(readBuffer, 0, _
                                        BytesRead - 2)

    ' We have a message so pass it on for processing
    RaiseEvent DataReceived(Me, Message)

    SyncLock client.GetStream
        ' Start a new asynchronous read.
        client.GetStream.BeginRead(readBuffer, 0, _
                                    READ_BUFFER_SIZE, _
                                    AddressOf StreamReceived, _
                                    Nothing)
    End SyncLock
Catch e As Exception
    ' Can add error handling code here
End Try
End Sub
```

The DataReceived event is raised, passing the instance of the broadcast, as well as the message received, back to the Windows Service.

```
Public Event DataReceived(ByVal tcpSender As TCPBroadcast, _
                          ByVal data As String)
```

As we have a link to the client held as an instance of this class we can send a stream of data back to the client using the SendMsg() method defined below. As with reading, we only send one message at a time, so we stop the asynchronous processing, build up a stream of binary data, and send it. Once all the data has been placed in the queue, we need to flush the buffer to ensure that the data is completely sent.

```
Public Sub SendMsg(ByVal data As String)
   SyncLock client.GetStream
     Dim writer As New IO.StreamWriter(Me.client.GetStream)
     ' Send the message
     writer.Write(data & Chr(13) & Chr(10))
     ' Ensure all the data is sent
     writer.Flush()
   End SyncLock
 End Sub
End Class
```

That is our client handling class built, so we can now move on to build the
Windows Service.

Remote Windows Service

As you saw with the TCPClient class, and as we discussed when detailing how
sockets worked, we need to build threading capabilities within the Windows Service.
This will allow the service to listen for client connections or messages coming in, and
pass these on to the relevant routines. We therefore need to import the
System.Threading and System.Net.Sockets namespaces within our remote
Windows Service to deal with this.

Before we detail this code any more, a brief discussion of threading is required. On a
single-processor machine, code is not actually running simultaneously, but neither is
code running in sequence. Applications each run in a different thread and the
operating system allocates a proportion of processing time to each one, which can
increase or decrease depending on whether the application runs in the foreground or
the background. You can create separate threads in your Windows Services that allow
you to move possibly long-running procedures to operate independently so that the
calling code does not have to wait for the procedures to complete before continuing.

Methods that are running in separate threads cannot return any value because no part
of the application would be waiting it for it. A new Thread object is created and the
address of the method is passed as an argument to its constructor. The execution of the
code is started by calling the Start() method on this Thread object and it will then
run independently of other code until it completes.

```
Imports System.ServiceProcess
Imports System.Threading
Imports System.Diagnostics
Imports System.Net.Sockets

Public Class LogMonitor
   Inherits System.ServiceProcess.ServiceBase

   Private ValidSource As Boolean = False
```

To listen to an event log on a computer, we need to set up Event Log object instances to deal with this. The Event Log methods and properties reside in the Systems.Diagnostics namespace, and through this we can listen for any entry created in a single particular log we choose.

```
Private EventLEType As New EventLogEntryType()
Private LogView As New EventLog()
Private NewEntry As AutoResetEvent
Private EventLogEntry As EventLogEntryType
```

It is also necessary to have our thread listener defined so that the Windows Service can deal with any threads that are executed, and we need objects to work with that.

```
Private Listen As TcpListener
Private ListenerThread As System.Threading.Thread
```

Finally the remote computer could have multiple clients listening in to this service. By having this multiple connection capability, several technicians can listen in at once to the event logs, which would cover scenarios of shifts, breaks, lunch, and so on.

```
Private Shared ClientsList As New ArrayList()

' Select a non reserved port to listen to
Const PORT_NUM As Integer = 24036
```

In the following OnStart() method, we first *spawn* a separate thread that the code of the DoListen() method will execute on. The DoListen() method will listen to client requests and react to them when they do appear.

```
Protected Overrides Sub OnStart(ByVal args() As String)
   Try
      ListenerThread = New Threading.Thread(AddressOf DoListen)
      ListenerThread.Start()
   Catch
      ' You can add some error handling code here, although
      ' nothing should go wrong here
   End Try
```

We also need to set up the event log for listening to the Application log. It is only Information type entries that will be dealt with, and although you cannot set a filter for this as this code is only run once, an object variable is set up for these types of entries here.

```
' Insert the log to use. This could come in through an XML
' config file, registry read, or wherever
Me.LogToUse("Application")
```

```
' We want to listen to information type messages.
EventLogEntry = EventLogEntryType.Information
```

This next section of code specifies the handler to use whenever an entry is written into the event log:

```
Try
    AddHandler LogView.EntryWritten, AddressOf EntryWritten
```

Now that the Event Log handler is defined and the specific log we wish to work with has been detailed, the service can now inform the system that it is ready to listen for events:

```
    ' This needs to be set to listen for events
    LogView.EnableRaisingEvents = True

    ' Set the thread
    NewEntry = New AutoResetEvent(False)
Catch ex As Exception
    EventLog.WriteEntry("Unable to add a handler " & _
        "for EventLog: " & ex.Message, _
        EventLogEntryType.Error)
    End Try
End Sub
```

When the service stops, we simply clean up after ourselves by closing connections and listeners.

```
Protected Overrides Sub OnStop()
    Try
        Listen.Stop()
    Catch ex As Exception
        EventLog.WriteEntry("Failed to stop listener: " & _
            ex.Message, EventLogEntryType.Error)
    End Try

    Try
        ' Stop the thread
        ListenerThread.Abort()
    Catch ex As Exception
        EventLog.WriteEntry("Failed to stop listener thread: " & _
            ex.Message, EventLogEntryType.Error)
    End Try

    Try
        If Not LogView Is Nothing Then
            LogView.Close()
        End If
    Catch ex As Exception
```

```
        EventLog.WriteEntry("Failed to close log " & _
            ex.Message, EventLogEntryType.Error)
      End Try

      Try
        If Not NewEntry Is Nothing Then
          ' Stop listening for events
          NewEntry.Close()
        End If
      Catch ex As Exception
        EventLog.WriteEntry("Failed to close Event Log " _
            & "monitoring: " & ex.Message, _
            EventLogEntryType.Error)
      End Try
    End Sub
```

In the OnStart() method of the service we called the following routine to set up the name of the log as well as the machine name of the log to monitor. If you had enough authority it would be possible to monitor a separate computer's event log. In this example this would be a bit meaningless as you would simply place this service onto that computer.

```
    Private Sub LogToUse(ByVal attachToLog As String)
      ' Check that what has been passed in is valid
      If LogView.Exists(attachToLog) = True Then
        LogView.Log = attachToLog
        ValidSource = True
        ' Attach to this machine as well.
        LogView.MachineName = System.Environment.MachineName
      Else
        ' Put out an error message here
        EventLog.WriteEntry("Invalid log " & attachToLog)
        ' Stop the service
        Me.OnStop()
      End If
    End Sub
```

Once an event log entry is written the handler listening out for this action will fire and process the following subroutine. Each log entry causes a thread to be created that passes in the event that has been created so that every property within an event is exposed for the system to use. By checking that the event is of the type we are looking for we will then broadcast this information to any client that is listening.

```
    Public Sub EntryWritten(ByVal source As Object, _
                        ByVal entry As EntryWrittenEventArgs)
      If entry.Entry.EntryType.ToString() = _
          EventLogEntry.ToString() Then
        Me.Broadcast(entry.Entry.Category & " " & _
```

```
                        entry.Entry.MachineName & " " & _
                        entry.Entry.Message)
        End If
    End Sub
```

It is this routine that will broadcast that information. Recall that we have a collection of
all the clients connected residing in a hashtable. By navigating each instance it is
possible to call the SendMsg method that is exposed in the TCPBroadcast class
library to send them broadcast.

```
    Private Shared Sub Broadcast(ByVal message As String)
        Dim client As TCPBroadcast
        Dim Item As Object

        ' For each client listening, send a broadcast message
        For Each Item In ClientsList
            client = CType(Item, TCPBroadcast)
            client.SendMsg(message)
        Next
    End Sub
```

During the service OnStart() method we set up a listener thread with a handler that
would fire when the thread was brought in to life. The following routine deals with this
by listening to the TCP/IP port within the WinSock sub system. Any connections that
are not based on that port are rejected but when a good connection does arrive, we
then build up the user connection and a link is established between the systems. We
can also now listen out for any data coming our way.

```
    Private Sub DoListen()
        Try
            ' Listen for new connections.
            Listen = New TcpListener(PORT_NUM)
            Listen.Start()
            Do
                ' Create a new user connection
                Dim client As New TCPBroadcast(Listen.AcceptTcpClient)

                ' Add an event handler to allow the user to communicate
                AddHandler client.DataReceived, _
                    AddressOf Me.OnLineReceived
            Loop Until False
        Catch ex As Exception
            EventLog.WriteEntry("Problems setting up the listener: " _
                & ex.Message)
        End Try
    End Sub
```

Any message that we do receive is processed here:

```
Private Sub OnLineReceived(ByVal sender As TCPBroadcast, _
                           ByVal data As String)
    Dim aCommands() As String

    aCommands = data.Trim().Split(",")
    Try
        Select Case UCase(aCommands(0))
            Case "NEW"
                ClientsList.Add(sender)
                sender.SendMsg("Connected")
            Case "LISTEN"
                Me.ListenOut()
                sender.SendMsg("Listening.....")
            Case "LEAVING"
                ClientsList.Remove(sender)
            Case Else
                sender.SendMsg("Unknown request. " & _
                    "Try New, Listen, or Leaving" & _
                    aCommands(1))
        End Select
    Catch ex As Exception
        EventLog.WriteEntry("Problems with message " & _
            ex.Message)
    End Try
End Sub


' Listen for events
Private Sub ListenOut()
    ' Pause for 2 seconds at a time for events in the event log
    Thread.Sleep(2000)
End Sub
End Class
```

Now that the service is built we need to add the installers. Insert an `Installer` onto the service but set the startup type to the default, `Manual`.

Installation

In the previous chapters, we looked at installing a Windows Service. We covered using the wizard, a setup project, and command-line installation. All of these options are perfectly valid for a remote installation as well, but it depends on the definition of remote.

In many cases, remote services will be developed for large organizations. Of course there will be several for smaller enterprises as well, but within all organizations, the network server administrators will be very protective of their computers, and will be extremely wary of any executable placed onto their machines. Its not so much the executable but all that comes with it. When building a setup project you will find it is not only your executable that attempts to install, but also other DLLs, potentially. These extra components may be more recent and up to date than any that already exist within the system32 directory, and therefore the setup program may overwrite these.

Therefore in probably the vast majority of cases, when you are writing remote services that will run on a server, you may find that the command-line InstallUtil.exe is the best solution. In addition, it does provide network server administrators with a simple and easy method of installing and registering a Windows Service; or they could use **Winstall** or Microsoft's own **Systems Management Server**, or **SMS** to help guide them through this process. To use remote installation, it is necessary for the server to have the **Remote Components** for .NET installed, thus making the server.NET compliant.

> *Winstall and SMS are utilities used by many organizations to control and remotely install applications, DLLs, services, etc. onto computers without the need of actually placing any installation programs on the system. There are other utilities that can complete a similar task.*

So now that we have our service built, copy the EXE to the system32 directory on a remote computer. In this directory, bring up a command prompt and install the service using the following instruction:

```
>InstallUtil /logToConsole=false LogMonitor.exe
```

Note that we have set the logToConsole option to false as it will be rare that you will want to see the actual install take place on a remote computer. Imagine the scenario that you are placing a service on every computer within your organization so that it will remotely monitor for viruses. As the service is installed, it would be disconcerting for users to perhaps see this installation take place. The whole install should be invisible to those users. If there was any problem with the install then you can still check the installation log.

This will install the service that you will be able to see on the remote computers' Services MMC It does this by inspecting the installers we placed within our application and the details there just as it would for a local service. You may well be presented with a dialog asking for a user ID and password that will be used by your service when starting. The dialog is shown overleaf with the administrator's account ID for the server that the service is being run on. You would only see this if you chose a User account type to be used for the Windows Service when defining the ServiceProcessIntaller component for the installer project. As we defined LocalSystem, then this dialog box is avoided:

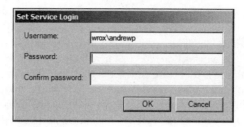

By then moving to the Services icon under Administrative Tools you should see the Windows Service installed.

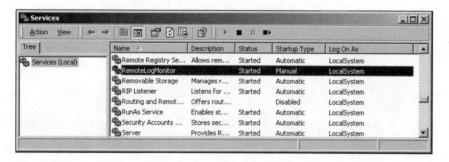

Most of the services do log on as LocalSystem, but it is not possible to put this account in the Set Service Login dialog. By moving to your service, double-clicking on it and then selecting the Log On tab, you can easily alter the service to a different username and password.

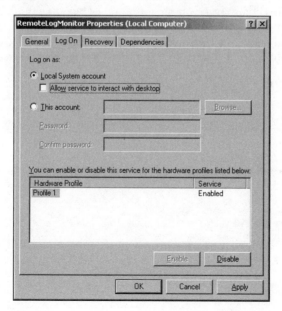

As we mentioned when building the service, it is crucial to know if the service install passed or failed. A moment ago we said that many remote services could actually be installed through a remote installation utility and it will be almost certain that the utility will not know if an install worked or failed as it will simply be looking for an end of the install itself, which unless there are problems such as being unable to connect to the remote computer or there was an unexpected error within your install code in the installer, the utility will be unaware of. So it is crucial to have some sort of post install check. This would mean looking through the install log and checking that the install was good.

So, now you should be able to deal with the installation of the service, so you can now build the project, place it on the server, and install it. Providing the install worked, then start the service and check in the Event Log that no errors have occurred. If you are running a firewall product then you may see a warning dialog come up informing you that a server has started and you should be aware.

Testing

In the following section we will build a simple form, TesterForm, which will reside on the client computer. This will send a connection to the remote computer and then just wait until the necessary event has been raised and passed across to us. We have detailed that we are listening for any event that is of an Information type. This is simply to allow easy testing of the service. You would place extra checks on the event log entry if desired to continue filtering any item so that you only received the correct entries.

So now that we know what to expect from the test harness, create a new VB.NET Windows Forms project and place on the form one listbox, MessagesList, and one command button, SetPropsButton. The form we will be building is using a large amount of technology that we have just covered in the Windows Service including TCP/IP, as you would expect. Therefore we will only cover the new ground as necessary.

```
Imports System.Net.Sockets
Imports System.Text

Public Class TesterForm
    Inherits System.Windows.Forms.Form

  Const READ_BUFFER_SIZE As Integer = 255
  Const PORT_NUM As Integer = 24036

  Private server As TcpClient
  Private readBuffer(READ_BUFFER_SIZE) As Byte
```

When the form loads we will create a client endpoint for the server using a new
TcpClient object with the predefined port. As we saw earlier we will receive a
TCP/IP connection if the connection is successful. We store this in an object variable to
be used for the communication between the two systems. There is no need to create a
collection of these, as we will only be listening to one server for events. Again, once
the connection is set up, we can wait for any messages being passed.

```vb
Private Sub TesterForm_Load(ByVal sender As System.Object, _
                            ByVal e As System.EventArgs) _
                            Handles MyBase.Load
  Try
    ' Set up a TCP client to the server.
    Me.server = New TcpClient("fat-belly-w2kas", PORT_NUM)

    ' Start an asynchronous read
    server.GetStream.BeginRead(readBuffer, 0, _
                               READ_BUFFER_SIZE, _
                               AddressOf BufferRead, _
                               Nothing)
    ' We would like to attach...
    Me.SendData("New, " + System.Environment.MachineName)
  Catch ex As Exception
    MsgBox("Server process is not active. " & _
         "Please try again. " & ex.Message)
    Me.Dispose()
  End Try
End Sub

Private Sub BufferRead(ByVal ar As IAsyncResult)
  Dim Bytes As Integer
  Dim Message As String

  Try
    ' Finish asynchronous read into readBuffer and
    ' return number of bytes read.
    Bytes = server.GetStream.EndRead(ar)
    If Bytes < 1 Then
      Exit Sub
    End If

    Message = Encoding.ASCII.GetString(readBuffer, 0, _
         Bytes - 2)

    Me.ProcessCommands(Message)

    ' Start a new asynchronous read into readBuffer.
    server.GetStream.BeginRead(readBuffer, 0, _
         READ_BUFFER_SIZE, AddressOf BufferRead, Nothing)
  Catch
  End Try
End Sub
```

As each received message comes in we will populate the listbox on the form so that we can monitor what messages are being received.

```
Private Sub ProcessCommands(ByVal message As String)
  ' Add in the message
  Me.MessagesList.Items.Add(message)
End Sub

' Send to the server
Private Sub SendData(ByVal msg As String)
  Try
    Dim writer As System.IO.StreamWriter
    writer = New StreamWriter(server.GetStream)
    writer.Write(msg & ControlChars.Cr)
    writer.Flush()
    writer = Nothing
  Catch
  End Try
End Sub
```

When the command button on the form is clicked, we are simply informing the service that the connection is made and we are ready to listen for any events.

```
Private Sub SetPropsButton_Click( _
    ByVal sender As System.Object, _
    ByVal e As System.EventArgs) _
    Handles SetPropsButton.Click

  ' Start listening
  Me.SendData("Listen,")
End Sub

Private Sub TesterForm_Closing( _
    ByVal sender As Object, _
    ByVal e As System.ComponentModel.CancelEventArgs) _
    Handles MyBase.Closing

  ' Leaving the server.
  Me.SendData("Leaving, " & System.Environment.MachineName)
  server = Nothing
End Sub
End Class
```

Build the project and then execute the form so that we can now test the service. Once you have started to listen to the service, it is necessary to generate some log events to prove the process. A simple way is just to close any of the other currently running services that are not crucial to the system. In the following screenshot a quick stop and start of Exchange Server brought up several messages to be sent to the client.

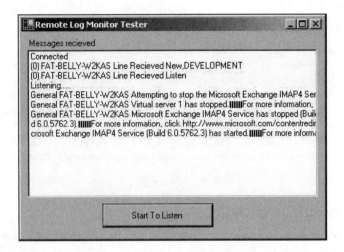

Now that we have looked at TCP/IP let's turn our attention to message queuing.

Message Queuing

Remote Windows Services in themselves are quite powerful utilities. As you have experienced in the previous example they can be used to silently monitor what is happening on a remote computer and give warning of potential trouble spots. It is possible to expand on services though, by using a queuing system to process requests in an orderly and timely fashion. This could be for using a Windows Service to install files onto a remote computer or handling transactions, such as share trading, when you are dealing with a WAN.

> *To enable queuing to perform on your server, it is necessary to have Message Queuing Services installed as a Windows Component. Without this you will find that the example we are going to build will not function. You can install Message Queuing Services as an option from your Windows CD/DVD. For this example to work MSMQ needs to be on both the client and the remote computer*

The example we will be building will be sending and receiving messages to and from client connections and processing these as necessary. We will discuss the application in more detail in a moment. But why do we need message queuing when it would be just as simple to call a method within a Windows Service?

MSMQ's Qualities

By using Microsoft Message Queuing as your method of communicating you are ensuring that every message sent to a Windows Service will be handled and dealt with in a robust fashion. Delivery is also guaranteed. What if you have a share trading system and perhaps there is a problem with your Windows Service or your database? The request to deal with trades would be lost as there was no current connection. However if there is a message queuing system built onto their server, all requests to trade would be held in a queue, whether the service was available or not, and dealt with in sequence when either the service caught up, or was available for trading once again.

MSMQ Requirements

We will be looking at MSMQ on a Windows 2000 Advanced Server installation. This is not a pre-requisite and could be any Windows operating system that has MSMQ installed. For the example to work, we need to create a queue on the remote computer, for the prices to come into. From Control Panel|Administrative Tools, select Computer Management and then navigate to the Services and Applications tab. From there you will see the Message Queuing node. Expand this and on the Private Queues sub-node, right-click and select New. This will bring up the Queue Name dialog box to enter the name of the new Private Queue. Enter TradingSystem and leave the Transactional box unchecked.

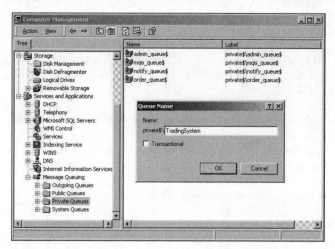

Once the queue is created, you then need to right-click on it and select Properties to set up the access rights, so that connected clients can place messages in the queue. In the Security tab add the necessary users that you wish to have access to this queue and give them permissions of Full Control. In a production environment you would lock this down more tightly, but this is a simple method of ensuring that whatever client login you are using, the queuing system will work.

Queuing Example

We are now going to take a look at a scenario where a Windows Service is being used as a trading system. There are many trading houses in the world where they are constantly buying and selling equities, loans, foreign exchange, and more, and they will use a central point for the trading to take place. The system could be local and within the country of the trading house, or it could be a system where the trading takes place remotely, such as in Milan with trading houses all around Europe. The crucial point is that the server with the process is not in-house.

This in itself throws up many issues like security, encryption, and so on. There are several methods that you can employ to ensure that your application remains secure, from using Virtual Private Networks (VPNs), through to tunnel software such as Altavista Tunnel. Both of these tools use a similar principle, which is to guarantee that there is a secure connection between two end points, either of which could involve a firewall.

Our application won't know this but we will be looking to create software that will mimic a trading system such as this. The basis of the system will be that several connections will be made to the Windows Service from different computers, and as they see fit, they will alter the price of a stock that is displayed. This will in turn send down this alteration to the Windows Service that will receive the request into its queue ready for processing. Once completed the new price would then be distributed to all the other clients using a similar system to that built in the earlier example.

Recording Actions

We will be using a very simple database structure for holding shares and recording price. There are two tables within the database.

- ❏   Shares – The share details such as name and price
- ❏   Share_Hist – The historical price of the share

This is not a database book so we are not going to worry about the design and the T-SQL code used to build this example. However what you do need to be aware of is the above tables. These two tables will demonstrate and prove how queuing will work when multiple actions occur and are dealt with in a synchronous fashion. Every time a share price is updated, which is one of the actions that we can have occurring in our service, an automatic record of the previous share price is made in the Share_Hist table. Enter the following code into a SQL Server database or the SQL Server desktop database MSDE. It is also possible to place this into an Access database instead, although we will be concentrating on SQL Server for this example.

> *If you don't have SQL Server then you can use EventLog entries to demonstrate queuing and read information from and work that way.*

```
SET QUOTED_IDENTIFIER OFF
GO
CREATE DATABASE [Traders]  ON (NAME = N'Traders_Data', FILENAME =
N'C:\Program Files\Microsoft SQL Server\MSSQL\data\Traders_Data.MDF' ,
SIZE = 1, FILEGROWTH = 10%) LOG ON (NAME = N'Traders_Log', FILENAME =
N'C:\Program Files\Microsoft SQL Server\MSSQL\data\Traders_Log.LDF' ,
SIZE = 1, FILEGROWTH = 10%)
 COLLATE SQL_Latin1_General_CP1_CI_AS
GO

use [Traders]
GO
CREATE TABLE [dbo].[Share_Hist] (
  [Share_Hist_Id] [bigint] IDENTITY (1, 1) NOT NULL ,
  [Share_Id] [int] NOT NULL ,
  [Price] [money] NOT NULL ,
  [Update_Time] [datetime] NOT NULL
) ON [PRIMARY]
GO

CREATE TABLE [dbo].[Shares] (
  [ShareId] [int] IDENTITY (1, 1) NOT NULL ,
  [Share_Desc] [varchar] (50) COLLATE SQL_Latin1_General_CP1_CI_AS NOT
NULL ,
  [Share_Price] [money] NOT NULL ,
  [Last_Update] [datetime] NOT NULL ) ON [PRIMARY]
GO

ALTER TABLE [dbo].[Share_Hist] WITH NOCHECK ADD
  CONSTRAINT [IX_Share_Hist] UNIQUE  CLUSTERED
  ([Share_Hist_Id])  ON [PRIMARY]
GO

ALTER TABLE [dbo].[Shares] WITH NOCHECK ADD
  CONSTRAINT [IX_Shares] UNIQUE  CLUSTERED
  ([ShareId])  ON [PRIMARY]
GO

ALTER TABLE [dbo].[Share_Hist] ADD
  CONSTRAINT [FK_Share_Hist_Shares] FOREIGN KEY
  ([Share_Id]) REFERENCES [dbo].[Shares] ([ShareId])
GO

SET QUOTED_IDENTIFIER OFF
GO
SET ANSI_NULLS ON
GO

CREATE TRIGGER ShareHist ON [dbo].[Shares]
FOR UPDATE
AS
```

```
BEGIN
  INSERT INTO Share_Hist (Share_Id,Price,Update_Time)
    SELECT deleted.shareid,deleted.share_price,GETDATE()
      FROM DELETED
END
GO
SET QUOTED_IDENTIFIER OFF
GO
```

We now need some basic information in our Shares tables just so we have some items to work with. Inserting the following information will give us the basic details we need. Again don't worry too much about the T-SQL code as we are simply putting some test data into the system.

```
INSERT INTO Shares (Share_Desc, Share_Price,Last_Update)
  VALUES('Jupitus Radio',17.98,GETDATE())
INSERT INTO Shares (Share_Desc, Share_Price,Last_Update)
  VALUES('Wilding Management',37.22,GETDATE())
INSERT INTO Shares (Share_Desc, Share_Price,Last_Update)
  VALUES('Jaffa Inc',5.32,GETDATE())
INSERT INTO Shares (Share_Desc, Share_Price,Last_Update)
  VALUES('Angry Automobiles',0.75,GETDATE())
INSERT INTO Shares (Share_Desc, Share_Price,Last_Update)
  VALUES('Julies Cakes',107.20,GETDATE())
INSERT INTO Shares (Share_Desc, Share_Price,Last_Update)
  VALUES('The Kids Club',1.48,GETDATE())
```

We now need to create a stored procedure that will be used to update the share price. By passing in the share ID and the new price, we can then update the share itself. Keep in mind that as part of our testing this will fire a trigger and will also update the Share_Hist table. By inspecting this table we will know that the messages have been processed in the correct order. As before, enter the following information into Query Analyzer and execute.

```
CREATE PROCEDURE updSharePrice @shareId int, @price money
AS
BEGIN
  UPDATE Shares
    SET Share_Price = @price,
      Last_Update = GETDATE()
  WHERE ShareId = @shareid
END
GO
GRANT ALL ON updSharePrice TO PUBLIC
```

Time to start working with MSMQ.

Message Queue Processor

Probably the greatest item you need to know when building an MSMQ application is that there should be a common DLL between the server and the clients that will be used to give a common interface to the data and the queue. On the client side, the DLL will be populated with the necessary information and marshaled by MSMQ over the network to the remote server where it will be placed in the predefined queue. So it is here that we start building our example.

> **When working with an MSMQ DLL it is vitally important that binary compatibility is kept at all times. Breaking this will give you no end of problems when it comes to rolling out the new solution. There will always be one or two clients running an old version of the system with the new DLL. Although Microsoft says DLL hell has gone, that's not quite true in this scenario.**

Create a new VB.NET Class Library project and name it MSMQReceiver. As we are going to be writing to the event log and working with SQL Server we need to import the relevant namespaces.

```
Imports System.Environment
Imports System.Diagnostics.EventLog
Imports System.Data.SqlClient

Public Class MSMQReceiver
    Private Conn As New SqlConnection()

    Private SQL As String
    Private SQLParms As New SqlParameter()
    Protected WithEvents SQLCommand As New SqlCommand()
    Private _ShareId As Integer
    Private _Price As Single
```

We use properties within DLLs to set values rather than Public defined variables. This keeps the interface cleaner and the integrity of the data intact. We will be using just two properties, one for the share ID that relates to the ShareId column in the Shares table, and one for the price we are updating.

```
    Public WriteOnly Property ShareId As Integer
        Set(ByVal value As Integer)
            _ShareId = value
        End Set
    End Property
```

```
Public WriteOnly Property SharePrice As Single
  Set(ByVal value As Single)
    _Price = value
  End Set
End Property
```

The following method will only be executed on the server. We will look at how it is executed when we look at the Windows Service, but essentially it is fired when a message comes into the queue. The messages are passed in as an object and we then perform a simple set of code to update the share price:

```
Public Sub ProcessMsg(ByVal msmqMsg As Object)
  Try
    SQLCommand.CommandText = "updSharePrice "
    SQLParms = SQLCommand.Parameters.Add("@shareid", _
        _ShareId)
    SQLParms = SQLCommand.Parameters.Add("@price", _Price)
    SQLCommand.CommandType = CommandType.StoredProcedure
  Catch
    EventLog.WriteEntry("MSMQReciever.DLL", _
        "Could not set parameters to update share price", _
        EventLogEntryType.Warning)
  End Try

  Try
    SQLCommand.ExecuteNonQuery()
  Catch
    EventLog.WriteEntry("MSMQReciever.DLL", _
        "Could not execute sproc to update share price", _
        EventLogEntryType.Warning)
  End Try
End Sub
```

In keeping with making the DLL generic, we have an interface for building the database connection. For the example we could have placed these details in a hard-coded setting specifically naming the server and database, but again this is demonstrating that server-side code does not simply need to be dealing with the incoming message.

```
Public Sub ConnectToDb(ByVal serverName As String, _
                    ByVal database As String)
  Try
    Conn.ConnectionString = "data source = " & serverName _
        & ";" & "initial catalog=" & database & ";" & _
        "integrated_security=SSPI;"
  Catch
    EventLog.WriteEntry("MSMQReceiver.DLL", _
        "Error in connection string", _
        EventLogEntryType.Error)
  End Try
```

```
      Try
        Conn.Open()
      Catch
        EventLog.WriteEntry("MSMQReciever.DLL", _
            "Error in opening connection", _
            EventLogEntryType.Error)
      End Try
    End Sub
  End Class
```

That's all there is to it. Of course, this is a very simple DLL and a business object would deal with scenarios such as trades occurring, broadcasting new prices and deals out to clients, and so on. We can now look at the Windows Service that uses this DLL.

Windows Service

As with the Windows Service in the first example, MSMQ uses threads to process incoming messages. Things are not as complicated as TCP/IP, as the System.Messaging namespace that deals with MSMQ protects us from a vast amount of background code. Create a new VB.NET Windows Service called RemoteTrader. Place the necessary installers and references into the project and then we can start coding. Once the project has loaded, move to the Components tab within the project and place a MessageQueue component on the design workspace and name it msmqQueue. Also add a reference to the MSMQReceiver project/assembly.

```
Imports System.ServiceProcess

Imports System.Messaging
Imports System.Threading
Imports System.Diagnostics.EventLogEntry

Public Class RemoteTrader
  Inherits System.ServiceProcess.ServiceBase

  Protected Overrides Sub OnStart(ByVal args() As String)
    Me.StartMSMQ()
  End Sub

  Protected Overrides Sub OnStop()
    Me.StopMSMQ()
  End Sub
```

This routine sets up the MSMQ connection and ensures that the Windows Service is ready to receive messages. The first action is to point the MSMQ object to the message queue we set up earlier using the object's FormatName property. You need to prefix the queue with the name of the computer on which the queue is. One performance gain to make is to have the actual queue processed on a server that is purely set up for this purpose. This will then avoid processing conflicts with any other applications being executed while messages are coming in. In the example below, the queue is pointing to the fat-belly-w2kas server. If you have the Windows Service on the same computer as MSMQ, then you could replace fat-belly-w2kas with a period mark denoting that the queue is local.

```
Private Sub StartMSMQ()
   Try
      If Me.msmqQueue Is Nothing Then
         Me.msmqQueue = New System.Messaging.MessageQueue( _
         "FormatName:DIRECT=OS:.\" _
         & "private$\tradingsystem")
      End If
```

Now that we have an object instance, the service can just wait for a message to arrive. Just as with the TCP/IP example the BeginReceive() method will wait asynchronously for a message to appear and hence is not stopping the Windows Service from executing. This is crucial as you may well be trying to stop the service for an upgrade or a new DLL. It would not be possible to do this if the service was indefinitely waiting for a message and that is all it was doing. There would be the extra problem of having to reboot the server after an installation removal. Note as well that there is no specific handler defined once a message is received. The MSMQ object has inbuilt events that can be utilized and we will come across one of those in a moment.

```
      ' Start waiting for messages to arrive.
      Me.msmqQueue.BeginReceive()
   Catch msmqExcep As MessageQueueException
      EventLog.WriteEntry("RemoteTrader", _
         "Problems starting queue " & msmqExcep.Message, _
         EventLogEntryType.Error)
   Catch ex As Exception
      EventLog.WriteEntry("RemoteTrader", _
         "Problems starting queue " & ex.Message, _
         EventLogEntryType.Error)
   End Try
End Sub

Private Sub StopMSMQ()
   Try
      Me.msmqQueue.Close()
      Me.msmqQueue.Dispose()

      Me.msmqQueue = Nothing
   Catch msmqExcep As MessageQueueException
```

```
        EventLog.WriteEntry("RemoteTrader", _
            "Problems stopping queue " & msmqExcep.Message, _
            EventLogEntryType.Error)
    Catch ex As Exception
        EventLog.WriteEntry("RemoteTrader", _
            "Problems stopping queue " & ex.Message, _
            EventLogEntryType.Error)
    End Try
End Sub
```

When a message is received, an event is raised internally with the MSMQ object once it has been received in full. This is very similar to what we had to do for the TCP/IP example with the exception that once again we have been protected from having to build the code that had to gather the stream of information together and then knowing when the stream had stopped. This makes message queuing a great deal easier to work with. Although there is the overhead of MSMQ installation and administration, from a development view point there is less code to worry about. The very first time you create a TCP/IP application it is tough to get it right the first time.

So the message is received and we now want to deal with it. We receive the message and place it into an MSMQ Message object that will allow us to inspect and work with the properties from the message itself. We then pass the body of the message in to our DLL that we created earlier and process the share price alteration after connecting to the database.

```
    Private Sub msmqQueue_ReceiveCompleted( _
        ByVal sender As System.Object, _
        ByVal msg As System.Messaging.ReceiveCompletedEventArgs) _
        Handles msmqQueue.ReceiveCompleted
    ' This event fires when a message is received.
    Try
        ' Get the message
        Dim msgMessage As Message
        msgMessage = msmqQueue.EndReceive(msg.AsyncResult)
        ' Cast the message body to an object instance
        Dim MsmqMsg As MSMQReceiver
        MsmqMsg = CType(msgMessage.Body, _
            MSMQReceiver)

        MsmqMsg.ConnectToDb("localhost", _
            "Traders")
```

Every computer has execution threads within it. Windows itself runs many threads, although as a VB programmer up until .NET, you may have only come across single-threaded applications. We won't get in to threading here as it is a large topic and there is a book available from Wrox called *Visual Basic .NET Threading Handbook* (ISBN: 1-86100-713-2), but in essence we are taking the DLL we have with the contents of our message and letting a pool of threads on the system process that message.

The computer will then deal with the work that is involved in the `ProcessMsg()` method but will move on and ready itself for any new message. This throws up many areas of concern. First of all, you cannot have a process used as a function with a return value. Secondly, you don't know when the thread will be executed so therefore you won't know what state the service will be in when you call back. Keep in mind that the work has to be self-contained.

```
        ThreadPool.QueueUserWorkItem(AddressOf MsmqMsg.ProcessMsg)
        ' Now continue listening for messages
        msmqQueue.BeginReceive()
    Catch ex As MessageQueueException
        EventLog.WriteEntry("RemoteTrader - MSMQ - ", ex.Message)
    Catch ex As Exception
        EventLog.WriteEntry("RemoteTrader", ex.Message)
    End Try
  End Sub
End Class
```

That's all there is to it. Build the project and place both the DLL and the Windows Service executable onto the remote computer. Do not forget to reference your DLL in the Windows Service project, otherwise you will get compilation errors.

We can now start building the test harness.

Testing MSMQ

A simple test harness based around a VB.NET Windows form application will suffice for the basic sending of a share ID and a price. There is no information returned to the client and the way of checking that data has altered is by looking within the `Shares` and `Share_Hist` table using a simple `SELECT` statement.

Name the form `TradersForm` and place two textboxes and a command button somewhere on it. It is necessary to place an MSMQ component on the form as well and set the `Formatter` property to `XmlMessageFormatter`.

Just as with the server-side code, we need to define the path of the message queue, the format the message will take when being sent across the network, and this time we need to give the synchronizing object to the MSMQ component. Yet again we are protected from the handshaking that is performed when a message is being passed across the network. By giving the message queue the object that is working with the queue, it can internally work with the process and `SyncLock` it as necessary, as you saw with the first example.

> *The reason that this is exposed in TCP/IP and not in MSMQ is that with TCP/IP there may well be instances where you want to be more in control of what is going on, for example if you were building an FTP client. With message queues you are quite simply building and sending a message and there is no need to know what is happening in the background.*

```
Imports System.Messaging

Public Class TradersForm
  Inherits System.Windows.Forms.Form

  Private Shared msmqQueue As System.Messaging.MessageQueue

  Shared Sub New()
    msmqQueue = New MessageQueue()
  End Sub

  Private Sub TradersForm_Load( _
      ByVal sender As Object, _
      ByVal e As System.EventArgs) _
      Handles MyBase.Load
    msmqQueue.Path = ".\private$\tradingsystem"
    msmqQueue.Formatter = New XmlMessageFormatter()
    msmqQueue.SynchronizingObject = Me
  End Sub
```

This last section of code is taking an instance of the MSMQ DLL we created a few moments ago, and setting the properties such that when it is marshaled to the server, the relevant information is contained within the message. Once we have set the details up, inform the MSMQ component by asking it to send the DLL by value, and not by reference to the queue.

```
  Private Sub NewPriceButton_Click( _
      ByVal sender As System.Object, _
      ByVal e As System.EventArgs) _
      Handles NewPriceButton.Click
    Try
      ' Create an object instance like normal
      Dim MSMQ As New MSMQReceiver.MSMQReceiver()
      ' Set some properties
      MSMQ.ShareId = CInt(Me.txtShareId.Text)
      MSMQ.SharePrice = CSng(Me.txtPrice.Text)

      ' Send it to the queue
      msmqQueue.Send(MSMQ)
    Catch ex As Exception
      MessageBox.Show("Problems updating Message Queue" & _
        ControlChars.CrLf & ex.Message)
    End Try
  End Sub
End Class
```

Execute the form and pass in a share ID and a new price. Then you can check the database by executing the following T-SQL against it and you should see your price alteration in place:

```
SELECT ShareId, Share_Price FROM Shares
```

Debugging

Debugging a remote Windows Service can prove much trickier than with a local service. First of all, you may be nowhere near the actual computer that is running the service. There may also be no Visual Studio .NET that you could even run the service as raw code with breakpoints in. You therefore need to make use of other methods. It is possible to pipe any information to the console but this is of no use if you do not have access to the screen. Perhaps the simplest method is to use the Application Log of the remote computer. By placing any errors within this log, with enough permissions granted on the server, you can connect to the remote log from your client machine and inspect the log from there. This is a simple and safe process, which removes the need to be running to and from your desk and the server room.

Before installing a service on a remote server, it is crucial and imperative that testing is completed either on a local computer or if you do need to actually remote the service, place it on a workstation that is next to you that by installing the service is not going to affect any user working on it. If you have to use a different computer, ensure that you have enough privileges on it, and that you keep the code within your start and stop processes to the bare minimum so that no matter what goes wrong, you can at least get the service to start and stop. There is nothing worse than a bad line of code either in the start, stop, or any of the other commands that stop, start or suspend a process that causes a problem. When this happens, the process remains in a state of limbo and quite often a reboot of the computer is needed.

This brings the next major point about developing and debugging a remote Windows Service. Until you are 100% certain you have a robust and secure Windows Service, always make the startup process a Manual action rather than an Automatic one. If the process is automatic, when you complete a reboot, the service will try to start running again. This could cause problems while you try to uninstall the service. If you come across the problem, then uninstall the service using the `InstallUtil.exe`, which will complain if it cannot stop the service, however, you will then find the service has gone when you next reboot.

In the first example we set up TCP/IP broadcasting. This was the first item to get working within the example so that I could use this method for debugging as well. If an error occurred, then by broadcasting the message back, it avoided populating the Application Log with error information each time an inspection occurred. Once the service was working, it was a simple process to remove the broadcast messages and build the release version of the service.

Finally, there is always the option of creating your own log in the Event Viewer for any messages to be recorded. The downside to this is that if every service and application did this, the number of logs would become very large indeed. If you find that your company is going to be building several services, then a `Services` log might be a good idea, as this would keep any entries out of the Application Log.

Summary

Remoting Windows Services does require extra design thought before even attempting to start building your solution. Whether you are using TCP/IP or MSMQ there is still some thought to be given to where specific processing should take place. Even deciding whether to use these two methods or Remoting itself is a design consideration. If there has to be any two-way interaction, then you really have to go down the TCP/IP route. Setting up queues on client machines as well as server machines is simply a maintenance nightmare and disaster waiting to happen.

VB.NET

Windows Services

Handbook

6

6

Scalability and Performance Issues

So far in the book we've discussed how to create useful and usable Windows Service-based applications. Now, in an ideal world we would have unlimited system resources to run our new Windows Service applications on. However, as we all know, it isn't an ideal world, and when we create applications (of any type), we often need to consider how to get the most out of the system resources available to us. In other words, we need to work out how to maximize the performance and scalability of our applications.

The number one rule of thumb when it comes to performance and scalability is: don't reinvent the wheel. For example, when you need a message queuing facility within your Windows Service, use the MSMQ provided rather than building your own. The chances that you could recreate the functionality that Microsoft Message Queuing provides are slim given the project deadlines we all are typically faced with.

Luckily, .NET provides us with several handy features for optimizing the performance and scalability of our applications. First, .NET's garbage-collection mechanism does a fine job of disposing of objects that are not needed anymore, freeing system resources. Second, we can enhance both scalability and performance by making our applications multithreaded. In this chapter we're going to show you how to improve the performance and scalability of Windows Service applications by looking more closely at both of these topics.

Using Threads

There are several ways to ensure that a service operates in a smooth and consistent manner allowing for reliable operation. This reliability includes performing its task with as little system impact as possible as well as being able to handle a much smaller or larger load on demand.

Creating a multithreaded Windows Service is one step to ensuring that your service performs well, and scales to meet needs down the road. Before you begin implementing a multithreaded Windows Service it's important to realize what multithreading is and where it may be appropriate to use this technology.

Windows has long been known as a multitasking operating system. The term "multitasking" means that Windows can run more than one application at a time. If you are like me, you typically have Visual Studio open, as well as an e-mail client, virus scanner, and any number of other applications at the same time during the normal course of a day. The fact that you are running all of these applications at exactly the same time means that – yes – your operating system can multitask; but when it comes right down to it, a single-processor machine can't actually run applications at exactly the same time. Windows, in common with most operating systems, employs pre-emptive multitasking. This simply means that each application and the threads associated with the application are allowed to run for a very small amount of time. After this amount of time, Windows yields time to another application to perform any processing it needs to do. This happens so fast and so often that it appears that all the applications are running in unison.

If you take a closer look at the applications you have running on your PC, we notice that most applications comprise several threads. Threads are somewhat analogous to fingers. Fingers perform work for us, can operate independently of each other, and share a body. Similarly, threads operate independently, perform work, and share process space. The fact that threads can operate in the background independently of the application that owns them gives them their strength.

Consider Microsoft Word. As you sit and type a document, you make spelling or grammar mistakes, and these items are underlined to denote that Word has detected a problem. As you type, Microsoft Word has created a thread that works in the background looking at everything you type, checking the spelling and grammar. This is done as a thread in the background because if Word were to pause each time you typed a letter just to perform spelling checks you would undoubtedly get fed up with the delay.

Another common use for threads would be a network server application, such as a telnet server. If you've ever written any networking application, you will know the frustrations that come with dealing with multiple connections at one time. Imagine trying to write your own telnet server that allows several hundred or even thousand users to connect to it. Without the use of threads you would need to keep track of all the connections, process the requests the users are imposing on your server (such as returning a directory listing), as well as sending feedback to the clients. This type of application without threads would quite possibly miss input from several clients because it was meeting the needs of other connections. However, if you were to create a new thread for each connection you would ensure that everything runs as smoothly as possibly. The pre-emptive nature of the operating system generally assures you that each thread will get processing time, allowing each connection to be served, and all the while sharing common information with the server application, such as security information.

These previous two examples provide excellent uses for free-threading in Visual Basic .NET. However, there are occasions when this approach may be a bit too much: you may only need thread queue functionality. For example, say you wrote an application that checks data in SQL Server and compiles sales totals, as well as projected amounts and miscellaneous other information. This application must also be able to retrieve this information upon request, as well as in a scheduled mode. Each of these operations can be assigned to a queue of worker threads. There are five threads in this queue, and ten operations that need to be completed. The threads complete the tasks, e-mail the results, and then take on another task as needed.

However, it is important to realize that by using a thread pool (queue of threads), the order that each task completes should be unimportant. All of the actions that need to be performed will get done, but in no certain order. Computing sales totals may have been the last thing added to the thread pool, but may finish a lot quicker than calculating projects sales for the month.

As you can see from the examples above, threads provide a means by which you can perform several operations at the same time on your computer, utilizing the massive amount of computing power available in computers today. Here we will cover some of the options available to us within Windows Services to help streamline these applications.

Controlling Thread Priority

Setting thread priority on a Windows Service helps ensure it gets ample time to perform its processing. Bear in mind, however, that if you increase the priority of a thread you are reducing the amount of time other processes receive from the operating system.

There are six different levels of priority:

❑ Low

❑ BelowNormal

❑ Normal

❑ AboveNormal

❑ High

❑ RealTime

The default priority for a Windows Service is Normal. If you have a processor-intensive application that doesn't need to run within a specified amount of time, you can set its priority to Low, which will yield more time to other running applications and processes. If, however, this application must perform calculations within a very short timeframe and on demand, it might be a good idea to change the priority to RealTime. An example of a RealTime Windows Service and/or application would be one that monitors vital statistics from hospital monitoring equipment. This type of application wouldn't typically be run on a PC with Windows and all the associated baggage that comes along with an operating system intended to be user-friendly. Most likely, this type of program would be on an embedded device running a specialized operating system such as Windows XP Embedded.

There is something else that you should note about thread priority levels:

> **There are six priority levels available from within the Windows Task Manager but the .NET Framework only gives us access to the bottom 5 levels.**

The Windows Task Manager gives us the ability to pick any running process and set the thread priority on that process. However, this isn't always beneficial, because it sets the priority for the entire process and not individual threads. When you create a multithreaded application by manually creating each thread, you have the option of setting a thread priority. To demonstrate the speed increase when these levels are altered in an application, look at the following code from a Windows Form Project:

```
Private Sub btnGo_Click(ByVal sender As System.Object, _
    ByVal e As System.EventArgs) Handles btnGo.Click
  Dim doSomethingThread As New Thread(AddressOf DoSomething)
  doSomethingThread.Name = "DoubleMath"
  doSomethingThread.Start()
End Sub

Private Sub DoSomething()
  Dim TTL As Double

  Dim i As Integer
  For i = 100000000 To 1 Step -1
    TTL = i * (i / 0.00234)
  Next
  MessageBox.Show("Done!")
End Sub
```

Here we have a simple Windows Form application with a button named btnGo. When the button is clicked, we declare a new Thread object and pass it the address of our DoSomething() method. The DoSomething() method will count from 100,000,000 down to one, all the while performing floating-point operations. Once the operation has completed, we display a message box to show that the thread has finished what it set out to do.

If this application is run on a Pentium III 450 MHz, it will take approximately 12.47 seconds to complete. Pretty quick for 100 million floating-point operations! However, if we return to the source code and add one line of code to adjust the thread priority, we can see what a major impact two thread priority levels can have on our code:

```
Dim doSomethingThread As New Thread(AddressOf DoSomething)
doSomethingThread.Priority = System.Threading.ThreadPriority.Highest
```

Now that the thread priority has been set to Highest, run the application again. The execution time should be around 7.71 seconds on a P III 450 MHz machine: in other words, by changing the priority of the thread, you can cut the processing time nearly in half. Try this test again, except when you click the GO button this time, move the application's dialog around on the screen. You'll notice that it will move, but there is a distinct lag in the system. This is because the system is offering the application thread more processing time than that of Windows Explorer, causing Windows Explorer to be less responsive. If you comment the thread priority line back out, you'll notice that moving the applications dialog around on the screen isn't a problem while it is performing the floating-point calculations.

This example was presented to you in the form of a Windows application, because it's much easier to perform benchmarking on a program that you can interact with than one that runs in the background. Therefore, when you are building a Windows Service, it's usually a good idea to test portions of processor-intensive code within a Windows Application project rather than within your actual Windows Service project.

You can set the priority for an entire process from within the Windows Task Manager by simply right-clicking on a process and choosing the Set Priority option. There are tools that will allow you to set the priority of a currently running thread, which we will cover later in this chapter.

Using Thread Pools

Multithreading a Windows Service ensures that multiple sections of code execute at virtually the same time. This is beneficial under circumstances where you must listen for data to arrive, receive data as it starts to arrive, and then process it once it has been obtained. You don't necessarily want to halt your receive method while processing data so you process the information in a different thread while waiting for more data to arrive. An excellent example of this would be a TCP server such as a web server or Telnet server.

While creating a thread, you need to consider many other issues beyond setting its priority and starting it. You must ensure that threads don't attempt to access the same data at the same time; you must ensure that one thread isn't waiting on another to complete, potentially causing a deadlock. A much preferable method for creating a multithreaded Windows Service is to use the System.Threading.ThreadPool class.

The ThreadPool class contains a virtual pool of threads available to .NET assemblies. You submit method calls to the thread pool and it handles the processing behind the scenes. The thread pool contains a dynamic number of threads. As you submit method calls to this pool, your method is assigned to the first available thread. If there are no threads available, the pool may create new threads or make your request wait until a thread has completed its operation. The default maximum number of threads available in the thread pool is 25 per processor – however this can be configured via the machine.config file.

However, before you set out to implement a thread pool in your application, you should consider whether you need it. Here are some scenarios where it is appropriate to use a thread pool:

❑   Demonstration applications

❑   Waiting for signaled OS Handles

❑   When multiple client requests are needed and order is unimportant (a web server, for example)

Here are some situations where you *shouldn't* be using a thread pool:

❑   When each thread will run for a long time

❑   If we need to set the priority of a thread (all threads in pool have the same priority and cannot be changed)

❑   If there are security concerns (new threads inherit security but not call context)

To show how we can use thread pools, we will take the Windows Service we created in Chapter 3, IISMon, and make a few slight modifications. The problem with the IISMon Service is that it only has the capability to monitor one server. With the help of the ThreadPool class, we could easily change the application to monitor several servers by submitting the monitor requests to this pool of threads. We could simply loop through each server name, checking each one in turn, but this could easily take a few minutes if you had a lot of servers to monitor. It's quite possible that before it checks all of the servers, the time could have elapsed in our timer again and it would have to start all over sending monitoring requests. By using the thread pool we are essentially checking all servers at exactly the same time.

The thread pool provides you with an excellent means to check the status of the World Wide Web Publishing Service on several servers. By using the thread pool, you cannot actually guarantee that the first item in the pool finishes before the second. In the case of IISMon, this doesn't really matter. What matters is that the servers are checked in a periodic manner.

Adding jobs to the ThreadPool is as easy as adding a WaitCallBack delegate to the pool's queue. The signature of a WaitCallBack() method must contain one input parameter of type Object and it must return nothing:

```
Imports System.Threading
Public Delegate Sub WaitCallBack(ByVal state as Object)
```

When the ThreadPool is ready to execute the method provided, it will assign it a thread. There are also members available to retrieve the total number of free threads in the queue in the event that you wish to wait to add it to the pool. Let's begin by building a new Windows Service solution called tpIISMon (thread pool IIS Monitor). The code for this entire project is shown here but we will only discuss the changes made since Chapter 3 that enable this Windows Service to utilize the thread pooling feature.

```vbnet
Imports System.ServiceProcess
Imports System.Web.Mail
Imports System.Threading
Imports System.Diagnostics

Public Class Service1
    Inherits System.ServiceProcess.ServiceBase

  Private Const monInterval As Integer = 300 ' Seconds
  Private Const svcName As String = "W3SVC"
  Private svcMachine() As String = {"POWERHOUSE", "DOTNETSERVER"}
  Private Const EmailTo As String = "brianpatterson@mchsi.com"

  Private m_cdTimer As Timers.Timer
  Private m_elEvents As New EventLog()
  Private m_NoticeSent As Boolean = False
  Private m_PeriodsDown As Long
  Public Shared m_MessageText As String

#Region " Component Designer generated code "

  Public Sub New()
    MyBase.New()

    InitializeComponent()

  End Sub

  Protected Overloads Overrides Sub Dispose( _
      ByVal disposing As Boolean)
    If disposing Then
      If Not (components Is Nothing) Then
        components.Dispose()
      End If
    End If
    MyBase.Dispose(disposing)
  End Sub

  Shared Sub Main()
    Dim ServicesToRun() As System.ServiceProcess.ServiceBase

    ServicesToRun = _
        New System.ServiceProcess.ServiceBase() {New Service1()}

    System.ServiceProcess.ServiceBase.Run(ServicesToRun)
  End Sub

  Private components As System.ComponentModel.IContainer
```

```vbnet
        <System.Diagnostics.DebuggerStepThrough()> _
        Private Sub InitializeComponent()
            Me.ServiceName = "tpIISMon"
        End Sub

#End Region

    Protected Overrides Sub OnStart(ByVal args() As String)

        m_cdTimer = New Timers.Timer(Me.monInterval * 1000)
        AddHandler m_cdTimer.Elapsed, AddressOf Me.OnTimerElapsed
        m_cdTimer.Start()
        m_elEvents.Source = "IISMon"
        m_elEvents.WriteEntry( _
            "IIS Monitor starting with an interval of " & _
            Me.monInterval.ToString() & " seconds.", _
            EventLogEntryType.Information)

    End Sub

    Protected Overrides Sub OnStop()
    End Sub

    Private Sub OnTimerElapsed(ByVal sender As Object, _
        ByVal e As System.Timers.ElapsedEventArgs)
        Dim ServerName As String
        Dim m_utl As Utility

        For Each ServerName In Me.svcMachine
            m_utl = New Utility(Me.EmailTo, Me.svcName)
            ThreadPool.QueueUserWorkItem(AddressOf m_utl.PollServers, _
                ServerName)
        Next
    End Sub

End Class

Public Class Utility
    Private m_EmailTo As String
    Private m_ServiceName As String
    Private m_SvcControl As ServiceController
    Private ServerName As String

    Public Sub PollServers(ByVal State As Object)
        Dim SvcStatus As System.ServiceProcess.ServiceControllerStatus

        ServerName = CType(State, String)
        Try
            Me.m_SvcControl = New ServiceController(Me.m_ServiceName, _
                ServerName)
        Catch se As Exception
```

```
        SendEmail(se.Message)
        Exit Sub
    End Try

    Try
        SvcStatus = Me.m_SvcControl.Status
    Catch se As Exception
        SendEmail(se.Message)
        Exit Sub
    End Try

    If SvcStatus = ServiceControllerStatus.Stopped Then
        SendEmail("IIS is currently down on server " & ServerName)

        Try
            Me.m_SvcControl.Start()
        Catch se As Exception
            SendEmail(se.Message)
            Exit Sub
        End Try

    End If
End Sub

Private Sub SendEmail(ByVal Message As String)
    Dim mmToSend As New MailMessage()

    mmToSend.From = Me.m_ServiceName
    mmToSend.To = Me.m_EmailTo
    mmToSend.Subject = "IIS Service Status: " & ServerName
    mmToSend.Priority = MailPriority.High
    mmToSend.BodyFormat = MailFormat.Text
    mmToSend.Body = Message
    SmtpMail.SmtpServer = "mail.mchsi.com"
    SmtpMail.Send(mmToSend)
End Sub

Public Sub New()
End Sub

Public Sub New(ByVal EmailTo As String, ByVal ServiceName As String)
    Me.m_EmailTo = EmailTo
    Me.m_ServiceName = ServiceName
End Sub
End Class
```

As you can see from the first few lines of the program, we have changed the
svcMachine variable to a string array. Now we can specify multiple machines to
monitor instead of just one. When the OnTimerElapsed event fires within our service,
we must perform a few steps to ensure we don't end up with deadlocks.

We will be using the For Each keywords to loop through all the server names we have defined within the application. The ServerName variable is the resting place for each machine name and will eventually get passed to the method used to actually perform the service monitor. Then you see that we declare a new class of type Utility:

```
Private Sub OnTimerElapsed(ByVal sender As Object, _
    ByVal e As System.Timers.ElapsedEventArgs)
  Dim ServerName As String
  Dim m_utl As Utility
```

This new class now contains the code that will actually use the service controller to check the World Wide Publishing service on each server, as well as our method used to send e-mail notifications. Each time we loop through a machine name using For Each, we must instantiate a new instance of the Utility class as seen here:

```
For Each ServerName In Me.svcMachine
  m_utl = New Utility(Me.EmailTo, Me.svcName)
  ThreadPool.QueueUserWorkItem(AddressOf m_utl.PollServers, _
    ServerName)
Next
```

There is a reason for this! If we were to call a local method to check the servers, each thread within our pool would receive a reference to the same method. Since all threads would be looking at the same method there is also a good chance that they would also contain the same machine names. Therefore, if we polled seven different servers, our service application would probably end up polling the same server seven times. That being the case, we instantiate a new Utility class each time, passing the name of the service and e-mail address to an overloaded class constructor (the New method). This ensures that each thread in the pool has a unique copy of the Utility class as well as unique data.

Once all server names have been iterated through and submitted to the thread pool via QueueUserWorkItem(), our service sits and waits until the elapsed time has expired again. You will also notice that we pass the name of the server in as the second parameter of the QueueUserWorkItem() method. This second parameter, referred to as a State object, can be any item the thread pool needs to execute the callback method correctly. Here we simply pass in a string value, and within the actual method that checks each server we use CType() to convert this State object back into a string.

If you take a look at the Utility class you will notice we made quite a few modifications to the code in the PollServers() method that actually monitors the Windows Services. First of all, unlike the example in Chapter 3, we are no longer keeping track of which services were once down and are now back up. Doing this would require us to keep a linked list of all servers, services, and the status of each of those services. You will also notice that we are a bit more conscious of errors and are using several Try-Catch blocks within the routine. I'm generally not so picky about intercepting errors – I've actually added these Try-Catch blocks to demonstrate the power of the thread pool.

As mentioned earlier, the thread pool by default has a maximum of 25 available threads. Adding 25 servers to monitor in this application shouldn't be a problem. But what happens when you want to monitor 26, 30, or even 100? Will it fail if we attempt to queue the request? No. I, unfortunately, don't have 30 individual machines here to test this application against so I simply typed in 30 random machine names. Our service will actually fail when it attempts to connect to the Service Control Manager of each of these machines (since they don't exist) but more importantly, when the failure occurs we should still receive an e-mail message from the application. As you can see, each Catch block contains a command to e-mail all error messages to the destination address:

```
Catch se As Exception
   SendEmail(se.Message)
   Exit Sub
End Try
```

By using this method we can prove that any items added to the thread pool over the limit of 25 will still execute, but execute when threads are available. Feel free to add the necessary installer to this Service application, and then install and run it. Once you have tried it on existing servers, give it the names of some non-existent ones. Try giving it the names of 30 servers. Once you've done this, you should notice 30 e-mails in your inbox. The first 25 will show up at practically the same time. Shortly thereafter you should receive the remaining notifications once threads are available and the thread pool is able to check those remaining five.

Debugging Multithreaded Applications

Debugging a multithreaded application requires a little more work than debugging a standard Windows application project. Throw into the mix that the application in question is a Windows Service, and a lot needs to be dealt with. The obvious feature to use here is the Attach To Process option of Visual Studio .NET. This will allow you to set break points and step through the code.

> **Stepping through each line of code within a Windows Service is highly recommended. Even if your service runs smoothly time after time, the chances are that stepping through each line of code after each major version change will yield some valuable insight.**

To demonstrate just how this works, let's debug the tpIISMon service we recently developed. Go into the PollServers() method and add a break point on the first available line of code.

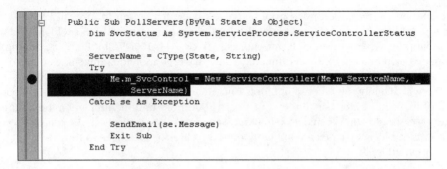

```
Public Sub PollServers(ByVal State As Object)
    Dim SvcStatus As System.ServiceProcess.ServiceControllerStatus

    ServerName = CType(State, String)
    Try
        Me.m_SvcControl = New ServiceController(Me.m_ServiceName, _
            ServerName)
    Catch se As Exception

        SendEmail(se.Message)
        Exit Sub
    End Try
```

Before we debug this service, it would be beneficial to change the poll interval so we don't have to wait five minutes for the event to fire. The time it actually takes to start the service and attach to the process can be upwards of 30 seconds on some machines, so let's change the poll interval to 60 seconds. With the interval changed, recompile the application and start the Windows Service.

Immediately after the service has started, from the Tools menu choose Debug Process (or press *Ctrl+Alt+P*). A list of running processes will appear. You will need to make sure the box labeled Show system processes is checked in order to see running services. Not only can we see a list of all the processes running on the machine, we can choose to debug processes on remote machines by selecting another machine from the Name: combobox:

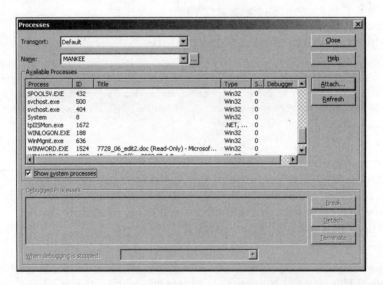

Scroll down in the list of processes until you find the tpIISMon service process. Once you find this process you can double-click it or click it once and then click the Attach button. With the service selected, you must now choose the program type that you wish to debug from the Attach to Process window.

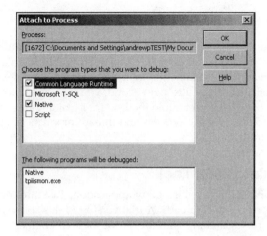

Our application is obviously running under the .NET Framework so click the Common Language Runtime checkbox. We haven't utilized any T-SQL or Script, but we do wish to debug native Win32 calls, so ensure that Native is selected as well. At this point you can click the OK button to attach to this process. While the debugger is attaching to the currently running process, you may notice in the background that Visual Studio is loading several symbol libraries for debugging purposes.

You should now be back at the Process list window. Now you have the option of actually breaking into the process and stepping through the code. Feel free to give this a try but I'm sure you get dropped into a long list of Assembly Language code since the process is quite possibly performing a function outside that of the .NET Framework and therefore outside the scope of our code. You will also notice on this screen that when debugging is stopped, the process we are currently debugging will be stopped as well. You can change this behavior by clicking on the When debugging is stopped combobox. For now close this Window.

After 60 seconds has elapsed, or whatever you set the poll interval to, you will reach the breakpoint and the process will pause allowing us to step through the code. As with any other application, Visual Studio .NET will display an arrow at the breakpoint indicating it is ready for user input.

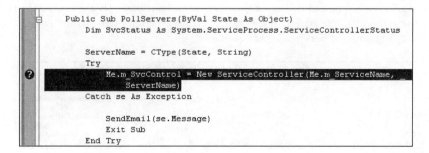

```
Public Sub PollServers(ByVal State As Object)
    Dim SvcStatus As System.ServiceProcess.ServiceControllerStatus

    ServerName = CType(State, String)
    Try
        Me.m_SvcControl = New ServiceController(Me.m_ServiceName, _
            ServerName)
    Catch se As Exception

        SendEmail(se.Message)
        Exit Sub
    End Try
```

At this point you are free to step through the code as needed, examining variables and such.

Attaching a service to a process and setting breakpoints works well if you need to examine the value of variables and perform other such simplistic tasks. However, if you want to view thread IDs, examine the memory requirements of each thread, or see how many times your thread executes per second, you will have a lot of work ahead in implementing the code. The preferable method for obtaining this information is by using a third-party tool that display process and thread information. Let's now take a look at one of these tools.

Using the TaskInfo 2002 Tool

In this section, we will examine a third-party application, TaskInfo, that allows you to examine in detail processes and threads. A trial version of this software can be found at http://www.iarsn.com/ or by searching with the various search engines.

TaskInfo allows you to monitor various aspects of threads and processes, including:

❑   CPU usage for processes and threads

❑   Context Switch Rates

❑   Physical and Virtual memory usage

❑   View and set process and thread priority

❑   All open files for a particular process or thread

❑   Extensive OS Information, including all loaded drivers

❑   Extensive hardware information

When it comes to monitoring a multithreaded application or Windows Service, TaskInfo is essential for any programmer's toolbox. To demonstrate its usefulness, we will use TaskInfo to monitor the tpIISMon service.

Upon starting the tpIISMon service, TaskInfo reveals that six threads were created for use by the service (note that the number of new threads will vary depending on your system). These threads are typical for a Windows Service that has been tagged as Apartment Threaded Model by use of the MTAThread attribute. Though you can't really access these threads, the .NET Framework has created them for reasons such as communicating with the Service Control Manager.

Process	▼ % CPU	LT % CPU	Time	Sw/s	InMem KB	Total KB	Th	Pri	Ver	State
tpIISMon.exe				0	6,400	73,292	6	Norm	4.0	32 Gui
-- Thread				0				8/8		Wait Executive
-- Thread				0				8/8		Wait User Request
-- Thread				0				10/10		Wait User Request
-- Thread				0				8/8		Wait LPC Receive
-- Thread				0				8/8		Wait User Request
-- Thread				0				8/8		Wait User Request

TaskInfo also reveals that the service is using approximately 73 KB of memory and is running with a Normal thread priority. A thread state of "32 Gui" indicates that the particular item is the main thread of the process and contains the message pump generally found within a Windows Form application. Even though we didn't specifically include a form within this Service, certain references were made by default within Visual Studio to provide this for us. In contrast, a state type of "32 Con" represents a 32-bit console application.

After a few minutes, your service will have detected that the IIS service is down. When this happens, TaskInfo will show you the new threads as they are created. In this particular instance, five additional threads (this number will vary depending on your system) were added to the thread pool as seen here:

Process	▼ % CPU	LT % CPU	Time	Sw/s	InMem KB	Total KB	Th	Pri	Ver	State	▲
tpIISMon.exe			0:01	1	11,448	99,072	11	Norm	4.0	32 Gui	
-- Thread				0				8/8		Wait Executive	
-- Thread				0				8/8		Wait User Request	
-- Thread				0				10/10		Wait User Request	
-- Thread				0				8/8		Wait User Request	
-- Thread				1				8/8		Wait Execution Delay	
-- Thread				0				8/8		Wait Event Pair Low	
-- Thread				0				8/8		Wait User Request	
-- Thread				0				8/8		Wait User Request	
-- Thread				0				9/9		Wait Event Pair Low	
-- Thread				0				8/8		Wait LPC Receive	
-- Thread				0				8/8		Wait User Request	▼

It's safe to assume that within the tpIISMon service, we are only using one additional thread at any given time; .NET has taken it upon itself to create a few extra threads for us – should we need them.

We will also find from the %CPU thread information that pops up sporadically that our Service application jumps from using virtually no processor time, to using a significant amount (in my case 20.5%). This really doesn't impact on the system since the service is currently running with a Normal priority and will yield to other applications that need time with the CPU. Once IIS has been restarted by our service application, if you continue to watch TaskInfo, you will notice the threads don't disappear immediately, but the threads will start to be removed one by one. During the author's testing, the six new threads were typically gone after an hour. Forcefully calling the Collect() method of the GC (Garbage Collection) class didn't seem to speed things up at all. Rest assured that the Service isn't leaking memory – .NET is just waiting to ensure the threads aren't needed anytime soon before it destroys them.

If you develop services that transmit or receive data over the network, TaskInfo is also capable of displaying transmission and receive rates as well. The author of this handy utility also assures that in future versions there will be enhancements for tuning multithreaded applications.

Sharing Processes

The .NET Framework and specifically the `ServiceBase` class allow us to create Windows Services that share process space with another service. The obvious benefit to this is that the services can share information without much effort on the programming side. We'll begin by building a project that contains two services: `Service1` and `Service2`. Each of these services will be in the same project and share process space.

Start a new Windows Service project within Visual Studio. Name this new project `MultiService`. The wizard generates a skeletal Windows Service for us as usual:

```
Imports System.ServiceProcess

Public Class Service1
    Inherits System.ServiceProcess.ServiceBase

#Region " Component Designer generated code "

  Public Sub New()
    MyBase.New()

    ' This call is required by the Component Designer.
    InitializeComponent()

    ' Add any initialization after the InitializeComponent() call

  End Sub

  'UserService overrides dispose to clean up the component list.
  Protected Overloads Overrides Sub Dispose( _
      ByVal disposing As Boolean)
    If disposing Then
      If Not (components Is Nothing) Then
        components.Dispose()
      End If
    End If
    MyBase.Dispose(disposing)
  End Sub

  ' The main entry point for the process
  <MTAThread()> _
  Shared Sub Main()
    Dim ServicesToRun() As System.ServiceProcess.ServiceBase
```

```
    ' More than one NT Service may run within the same process. To add
    ' another service to this process, change the following line to
    ' create a second service object. For example,
    '
    '    ServicesToRun = _
    '        New System.ServiceProcess.ServiceBase() {New Service1, _
    '        New MySecondUserService}
    '
    ServicesToRun = _
        New System.ServiceProcess.ServiceBase() {New Service1}

    System.ServiceProcess.ServiceBase.Run(ServicesToRun)
  End Sub

  'Required by the Component Designer
  Private components As System.ComponentModel.IContainer

  ' NOTE: The following procedure is required by the
  ' Component Designer
  ' It can be modified using the Component Designer.
  ' Do not modify it using the code editor.
  <System.Diagnostics.DebuggerStepThrough()> _
  Private Sub InitializeComponent()
    components = New System.ComponentModel.Container()
    Me.ServiceName = "Service1"
  End Sub

#End Region

  Protected Overrides Sub OnStart(ByVal args() As String)
    ' Add code here to start your service. This method should set things
    ' in motion so your service can do its work.
  End Sub

  Protected Overrides Sub OnStop()
    ' Add code here to perform any tear-down necessary
    ' to stop your service.
  End Sub

End Class
```

As you can see in the wizard-generated code, there is one particular line of code that allows us to insert more than one Windows Service into this project and thus into this process. The ServiceBase is accepting one particular service class in the generated code, but in the comment just before, you can see that you also have the option of passing in an array of ServiceBase objects. By doing this, when the above service is installed and started, both services are actually instantiated. Even though they are both instantiated, only Service1 has actually started. To expand on this let's add a new Component class file object to this project. This can be done in Visual Studio .NET by clicking on the Project menu and selecting Add New Item. Once the Add New Item window appears, select Component Class and name the file Service2.vb.

This new Component Class will essentially contain the same code as the wizard-generated code, with the exception of the defined class and service names. Place the following code within this file:

```
Imports System.ServiceProcess

Public Class Service2
    Inherits System.ServiceProcess.ServiceBase

#Region " Component Designer generated code "

  Public Sub New()
    MyBase.New()

    ' This call is required by the Component Designer.
    InitializeComponent()

    ' Add any initialization after the InitializeComponent() call

  End Sub

  'UserService overrides dispose to clean up the component list.
  Protected Overloads Overrides Sub Dispose( _
      ByVal disposing As Boolean)
    If disposing Then
      If Not (components Is Nothing) Then
        components.Dispose()
      End If
    End If
    MyBase.Dispose(disposing)
  End Sub

  ' The main entry point for the process
  <MTAThread()> _
  Shared Sub Main()
    Dim ServicesToRun() As System.ServiceProcess.ServiceBase

    ServicesToRun = _
      New System.ServiceProcess.ServiceBase() {New Service2()}

    System.ServiceProcess.ServiceBase.Run(ServicesToRun)
  End Sub

  'Required by the Component Designer
  Private components As System.ComponentModel.IContainer

  ' NOTE: The following procedure is required by the
  ' Component Designer
  ' It can be modified using the Component Designer.
  ' Do not modify it using the code editor.
  <System.Diagnostics.DebuggerStepThrough()> _
  Private Sub InitializeComponent()
```

```
      components = New System.ComponentModel.Container()
      Me.ServiceName = "Service2"
  End Sub

#End Region

  Protected Overrides Sub OnStart(ByVal args() As String)
  ' Add code here to start your service. This method should set things
  ' in motion so your service can do its work.
  End Sub

  Protected Overrides Sub OnStop()
  ' Add code here to perform any tear-down necessary to
  ' stop your service.
  End Sub

End Class
```

Now that you have added a new service to this project, you will need to modify a line of code within the Main() method, located in the Service1.vb file. Change the line as seen here:

```
Shared Sub Main()
  Dim ServicesToRun() As System.ServiceProcess.ServiceBase

  ' More than one NT Service may run within the same process. To add
  ' another service to this process, change the following line to
  ' create a second service object. For example,
  '
  '    ServicesToRun = _
  '        New System.ServiceProcess.ServiceBase () {New Service1, _
  '        New MySecondUserService}
  '
  ServicesToRun = _
      New System.ServiceProcess.ServiceBase() {New Service1(), _
      New Service2()}

  System.ServiceProcess.ServiceBase.Run(ServicesToRun)
End Sub
```

When the service is executed, both Service1 and Service2 will be instantiated. As usual, you must add a service installer before you can test the service. You add this installer to both Service1 and Service2. From within Visual Studio .NET, click on the Service1.vb file in Solution Explorer. Click on the Add Installer hyperlink in the Property window of each service. Once the code has been generated, click on the Service2.vb file and add an installer there as well.

Now you have your services and installers. What you haven't done at this point is name the services to identify them in the Event Log. To change the names of the services, double-click the `ProjectInstaller.vb` file that was added by Visual Studio. By double-clicking this you will be able to view the three objects that were created when you clicked the Add Installer link:

The names of the services are contained within the `ServiceInstaller` objects. Click the `ServiceInstaller1` object. Ensure the `ServiceName` property for this object is set to `Service1`. The `DisplayName` property for this object should be set to `MultiService1`. Then click on `ServiceInstaller2` and set the `ServiceName` property to `Service2`. Set the `DisplayName` property to `MultiService2`:

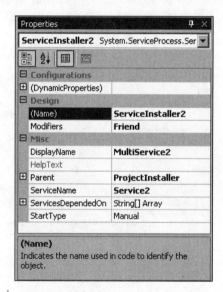

Also click the `ServiceProcessInstaller` object and change the `Account` property to `LocalSystem`. This will let our service run with more than enough privileges and doesn't require us to create a user account for merely testing an application. Install this new service using the `InstallUtil` application:

```
> installutil MultiService.exe
```

Once the service has been successfully installed, you can examine just how multiple Windows Services can run within the same process.

158

Memory Management

The .NET Framework boasts a garbage-collection facility that provides memory management for the programmer. The programmer is free to code and not worry about such things as reference counting, circular reference leaks, or dangling references. However, just because garbage collection handles memory issues for you, there are things to keep in mind when building an application that needs to provide 24 x 7 uptime. In this section we will cover the basic operation of the garbage collection class (System.GC) as well as best practices for managing your memory.

.NET Framework Types

The .NET Framework contains two specific types: value types and reference types. The type of an instance greatly affects how it is managed in memory by the .NET Framework. When using value types, each instance is stored in memory that has been allocated on the stack. Since value types are always accessed directly, it would be impossible for you to create a reference to a value type. Since you cannot create a reference to the instance of a value type that has been deallocated there is no possibility of creating a dangling reference to a value type.

Memory for a value type is deallocated when the scope activation record for the type has been removed from the stack.

Reference types are managed objects that you can create by calling the New operator. Memory is managed for reference types on the CLR managed heap. When accessing "managed objects" you must use a reference to the storage. When references are used, the garbage-collection facility is able to track these references and when they are no longer used, it is free to remove them from the memory heap. Since reference types can only be released through garbage collection when there are no longer any reachable references to the object, you can be assured that there are no dangling references to objects throughout the execution of your application.

The Garbage Collection Process

Garbage collection generally occurs behind the scenes without intervention. For those impatient programmers out there, the GC class also exposes a Collect() method to invoke the collection process as needed. In any event, when garbage collection occurs, it looks for and removes any objects in the heap that are no longer in use. If garbage collection succeeds and finds enough objects within the heap that can be freed, new objects can be created and allocated. If enough memory for new objects cannot be freed, an OutOfMemoryException is thrown.

By examining the steps garbage collection takes to find and remove free objects from memory, we can better understand where problems will arise in applications that should be extremely memory friendly and allow for extended up-times.

1. Garbage collection waits until all threads within an application have reached a safe point before it attempts to locate and remove unused objects. A safe state for a thread would be considered "suspended". Therefore, if you write an application that uses many background processor-intensive threads, you can rest assured that garbage collection will be few and far between. Threads within Windows Service applications should be implemented as the smallest unit of work possible and deal with the least number of objects possible. If the thread is processor intensive this will ensure that its memory utilization is minimal.

2. Garbage collection then creates a graph of all reachable objects. This is done by adding all objects to the graph that are contained within an application's root reference. It then recursively adds objects contained within each root-referenced object. This is very similar to Java's "reachable".

3. Garbage collection then compacts the heap by moving all reachable objects. When reachable objects are moved down within the heap, it then reclaims space used by unreachable objects.

4. References to all reachable objects within the heap are then updated in the application.

> **Threads within Windows Service applications should be implemented as the smallest unit of work possible and deal with the least number of objects possible. If the thread is processor intensive this will insure that its memory utilization is minimal.**

The .NET Framework also provides features that allow an object to be notified before it is destroyed. This allows the object to clean up before it is released from memory. Taking advantage of this can greatly enhance the performance of memory-intensive applications.

Finalization

Many objects contained within the .NET Framework contain a `Finalize()` method. The method is called when there are no longer any valid references to the object. The act of calling the `Finalize()` method is know as **finalization**.

The `Finalize()` method should only be used to clean up unmanaged resources. Unmanaged resources cannot be cleaned up by the garbage-collection class, so they need a point in an application that allows them to free memory before the object that instantiated them is cleaned up as well. With this in mind, let's take a look at two classes:

```
Class ClassA
    Private m_clsB as Object

    Public Sub New()
        Me.m_clsB = new ClassB
    End Sub
    Protected Overrides Sub Finalize()
        Me.m_clsB = Nothing
    End Sub
End Class

Class ClassB
    Public Sub New()
        ' Do Something?
    End Sub
End Class
```

From this example you can see that the ClassA class instantiates a ClassB object. ClassA may only use this object for a short time. However, in the Finalize() method of ClassA, you can see there is a reference to ClassB. This means that if you use the ClassB object for a short period of time, garbage collection won't free the memory that has been allocated to it because there is still a reference to it. If you were to place all object references in your Finalize() method, none of the objects listed there would be freed until garbage collection actually processes ClassA. You could potentially have hundreds upon hundreds of objects sitting around for no apparent reason. This could be disastrous in an application that runs for extended periods of time. The outcome of this is:

> **Never reference managed objects within a Finalize() method.**

Summary

In this chapter we walked through the general principles of implementing threads and thread pools within a Windows Service Application.

We saw that not only can multithreaded applications lead to a more responsive application, but they help break work units up into more distinct pieces of your software puzzle. These software puzzle pieces can help a great deal when it's time to debug your application. For a complete picture on building a multithreaded application you may find Wrox' *Visual Basic .NET Threading Handbook* (ISBN 1-86100-713-2) an invaluable reference.

You also learned some key points about managing memory associated with your services. Though .NET's garbage collection should work for you in freeing up memory, it is up to the programmer to use objects correctly so that the GC class can do its job as efficiently as possible.

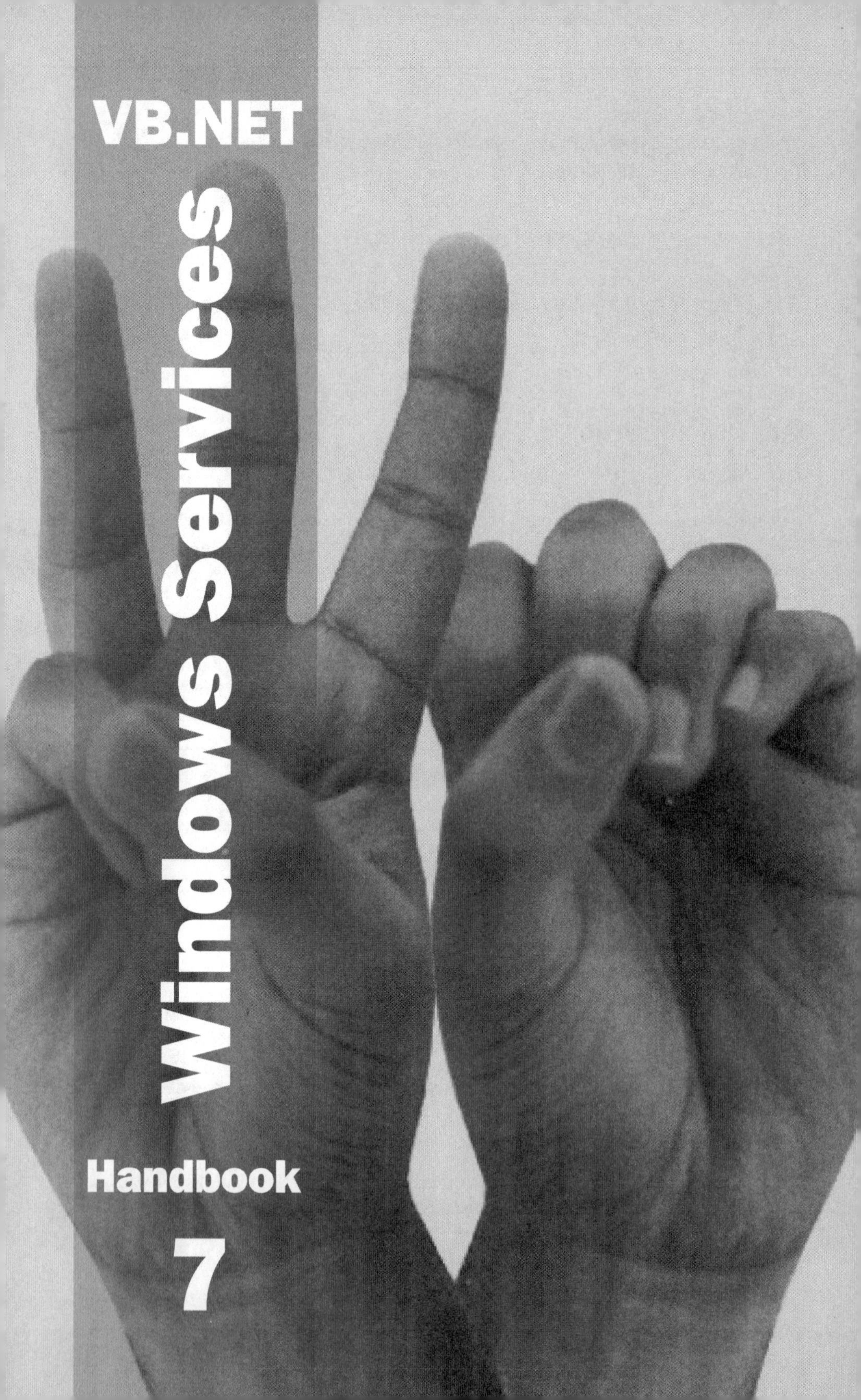
VB.NET
Windows Services
Handbook
7

7

Deploying Windows Services

So far we've spent a lot of time discussing Windows Service application design and development. However, if we want other users to be able to make use of our new application, the work doesn't stop once we've finished developing (and debugging). We need to consider how we are going to package up our application in a way that makes it easy to distribute and install (deploy) on other machines.

There are various ways to approach deployment. You could simply supply a batch file with compressed files and let the user handle details such as actually registering the service and configuring the access rights. However, this approach enhances the possibility of a user error, resulting in a failed installation. A better (more user friendly) approach is to build an installation application that handles all of the more complex deployment details for the user, making your Windows Service application easier to install and more professional.

In this chapter you will learn to create a fully featured deployment project for a Windows Service. This deployment project will be capable of automatically installing and registering a Windows Service application, as well as uninstalling the service.

We will finish the chapter by looking at the Windows Service Database, a useful source of information about the Windows Services installed on a system.

Operating System Issues

At the moment, only Windows NT 4.0, Windows 2000, Windows XP, and Windows .NET Server support Windows Services. This isn't because Microsoft was being picky about what should and should not allow a service, but rather because Windows 9x-based operating systems lack kernel functionality to allow such activities, and also lack a security context.

It goes without saying that building and using a Windows Service will involve you meeting certain needs. The machine that hosts the service needs to have a high percentage of uptime, and you need an operating system that is geared towards server applications. Windows 9x-based operating systems definitely do not fall into this category. Therefore, the logical choice is an NT-based kernel that has all of these attributes and more.

Adapting to the OS

The features supported among the various NT-based operating systems are essentially the same, so when it comes to dealing with Windows Services you really won't experience any compatibility issues as far as the deployment is concerned. There are certain things, such as a few security contexts, that aren't supported on older operating systems such as Windows 2000 and Windows NT 4.0. However, as long as you stick with User or System Service, you will be in good shape.

You might also find it a good practice to determine the type of security context to use within the code to your service. By simply using a dozen lines of code, you can quickly determine what operating system you are running on. A practical purpose for this would be to create a Windows Service application that has a Windows Form mode to it. When you install your service on an NT-based operating system, it would install and run as a typical service. However – if your application determines that it is running on Windows 95, Windows 98, or Windows ME, it could run in the system tray as a typical Windows Forms application.

I typically place this kind of code in a `Utility` class, as seen here:

```
Public Class Utility
    Public Function OSName() As String
        Dim OSInfo As OperatingSystem = Environment.OSVersion
        Dim VInfo As Version = OSInfo.Version
        Dim ID As System.PlatformID = OSInfo.Platform
        Dim MajV As Integer = VInfo.Major
        Dim MinV As Integer = VInfo.Minor

        If ID.ToString() = "Win32Windows" And MajV >= 4 And MinV = 0 Then
            Return "Windows 95"
        End If

        If ID.ToString() = "Win32Windows" And MajV >= 4 _
            And MinV > 0 And MinV < 90 Then
            Return "Windows 98"
        End If

        If ID.ToString() = "Win32Windows" And MajV >= 4 _
            And MinV > 0 And MinV >= 90 Then
            Return "Windows ME"
        End If
        If ID.ToString() = "Win32NT" And MajV <= 4 And MinV = 0 Then
            Return "Windows NT"
```

```
      End If
      If ID.ToString() = "Win32NT" And MajV = 5 And MinV = 0 Then
         Return "Windows 2000"
      End If
      If ID.ToString() = "Win32NT" And MajV = 5 And MinV > 0 Then
         Return "Windows XP"
      End If
      Return "Unknown OS"
   End Function
End Class
```

Simply call the OSName() method and it returns a string indicating the current operating system. You can, from this point, make adjustments in your service to meet special OS needs.

Supported Features

Deploying Windows Services with the Setup and Deployment project feature of Visual Studio .NET allows for a great deal of control during the installation process. You can perform custom actions during any phase of the installation, which might include registering the assembly as a Windows Service, launching a web page or external application, or parsing Registry keys and performing conditional operations based on those keys.

Many third-party installation utilities allow for extremely complex installations. Basing your installation around one of these third-party tools will give you greater flexibility than writing your own installation routine, but it generally takes more time because knowledge of proprietary scripting languages is required. When you just need to create a simple installation with only a few custom actions, you can accomplish this literally within a few minutes using Visual Studio .NET. You can also modify and add to any of the dialogs that are displayed during the process.

Installing and Uninstalling

Installation of a Windows Service is very straightforward. You can use the provided command-line tools – such as XCopy and InstallUtil – to do the job, or you can create installation routines that take care of everything for you, as we will see very shortly.

Using the InstallUtil Tool

The installation tool provided with the .NET Framework SDK, InstallUtil.exe, allows you to install and uninstall applications by accessing installer components within the assembly. The installation utility can be invoked from a console window, which is typically easier when testing Windows Services.

To install a Windows Service, you must ensure that you have added an installer to the solution, and then type the following command:

> **installutil <assemblyname>**

Referring back to Chapter 3, we created a Windows Service called `IISMon.exe`. Installing that particular assembly so it is registered and recognized as a Windows Service is as easy as:

> **installutil iismon.exe**

To uninstall the service you simply need add the /u switch before the assembly name.

> **installutil /u iismon.exe**

Instead of using the /u switch, you may also specify the full switch /uninstall.

The installation tool is actually a very simple .NET application. By using the Intermediate Language Disassembler (ILDASM) tool you can see that the installation utility merely makes a call to the `InstallHelper()` method of the `System.Configuration.Install.ManagedInstaller` class. Don't bother taking the time to look this method up in the help file, as it merely states that this method is used for support of the .NET Framework. No additional information is provided.

By using ILDASM, it is obvious that this `InstallHelper()` method accepts one parameter, a string array. This string array contains the same information that is passed into the `InstallUtil` application. Therefore it is safe to assume that passing the name of your assembly or /u and the name of your assembly to this method will yield the same results as actually using the `InstallUtil` console application.

Aside from the /u switch, there are a few more options available to you when using `InstallUtil`. The switches and their functionality are detailed in the table below:

Switch	Description
/AssemblyName	This parameter will be interpreted as an assembly name. By default, this is interpreted as the filename of the assembly you wish to install or uninstall.
/LogFile	This switch allows you to specify where installation results are logged. If you do not specify this parameter, no log file will be created. The default name for a log file is `<assemblyname>.InstallLog` This log file is created in the same directory as the `InstallUtil` application.

Switch	Description
/LogToConsole	The default for this switch is TRUE. If set to FALSE, then all output to the console will be suppressed.
/ShowCallStack	Showing the call stack is very helpful if you ever encounter an exception while installing or uninstalling an assembly. By specifying this switch, the call stack will be added to the log should an exception occur.

Using Deployment Projects

As you can see, the installation utility has a number of switches to allow you great control over the installation process and to track what went wrong when an installation fails. All of these features are great for development purposes, but when you actually distribute a Windows Service it's best to create a **deployment project** to handle the tasks for you. Deployment projects not only allow you to copy the binaries to a target machine, but the assembly can automatically be registered as a Windows Service as well. The person performing the installation shouldn't have to be familiar with the various .NET tools needed to register these types of projects, and automating this removes a probable point of failure during installation. A deployment project also allows you to create any necessary icons on the target system, and to perform checks on software and hardware components should your service application have special needs.

Visual Studio provides us with a Setup and Deployment project that not only distributes Windows Forms applications and Web Applications, but also distributes, installs, and registers Windows Services.

Creating a Deployment Project

Let's take a look at some of these features by creating an installation for the IISMon service we created in Chapter 3. From the File menu in Visual Studio .NET choose New | Project, then from the Project Type list choose Setup and Deployment Projects. Next choose the Setup Wizard template, and name this new project MonInstall, as in the following screenshot:

After you have entered in the name of this project, click the OK button. The Setup Wizard will then open with some general information. Click the OK button when the Wizard opens. You will then be asked what kind of setup you wish to create. We want to build a setup for a Windows application, so ensure that the first radio button is selected, as shown here:

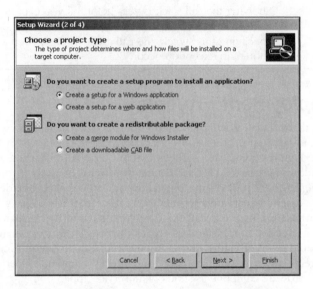

Now click the Next button. Next you need to add all of the files that you wish to distribute in this deployment project. In our case, the IISMon Windows Service requires only one file, the executable itself. Click the Add button and navigate to the location where you built the IISMon assembly. Select the executable and then click OK.

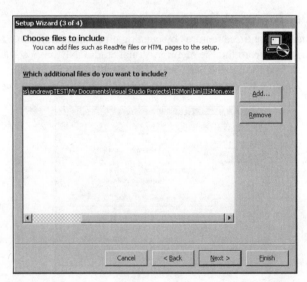

Once you have selected the file and added it to this project, you will see the name of the file and location shown within this window. If there are any additional files you wish to distribute, such as a configuration or Readme file, you should add them too in this step. Once a file is added, the Setup Wizard scans the assembly for dependency information. Any dependencies that are needed, with the exception of the .NET Framework itself, are added to the resulting solution for distribution as well. At this point we can click the Next button, and our new project appears with the Visual Studio Environment.

When Visual Studio displays the project, you will notice several key windows full of information. The main panel contains a representation of the file system. This file system layout displays the files that need to be distributed, as well as any shortcuts we wish to add to the Start menu or desktop. The Solution Explorer displays the IISMon.exe application and the dependency information that was retrieved from the assembly.

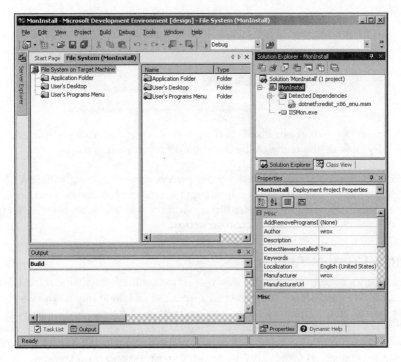

As you can see, the only dependency is that on the .NET Framework itself. However, the small circle with a line through it means that the Framework itself will not be distributed within the setup that we are in the process of creating. It is important to note that as the .NET Framework won't be included in the installer, machines that do not have the Framework installed cannot use the service. A way around this is to include the dotnetfx.exe program in the installation program. This will install the "skinny" version of the .NET Framework, which is the minimal version of the Framework that is needed in order to run a .NET Service.

You will also see several properties in the Properties window for this project. The properties include product information, as well as the name of the author and manufacturer. Before we move on, change both the `ProductName` and `Title` properties to "IIS Monitor":

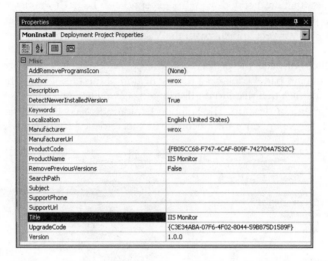

This will ensure that when our installation runs the correct application name is displayed. By default, the name of the installation project is displayed.

At the moment we are at the stage where our project will create an installation file that will distribute the `IISMon` application to a target machine. However, one important process is missing: we need to register the application as a Windows Service. To achieve this we will need to add a **custom action**.

Adding a Custom Action

To add a custom action, click on the View menu from within Visual Studio .NET and choose Editor. We then choose Custom Actions from the cascaded menu. The Custom Actions editor will then open, showing us a treeview with four nodes; each node within this treeview represents a point in the installation process. By placing a custom action within each of these nodes, actions can be performed as different phases of the installation procedure. These phases are Install, Commit, Rollback, and UnInstall:

Install Phase	Description
Install	The Install phase begins the installation process. Once the Install phase has completed, Commit is then called to complete the installation.
Commit	Commit is called once an installation has completed successfully. This completes the installation transactions.

Install Phase	Description
RollBack	RollBack is the phase of installation that occurs when an installation has failed for one reason or another. RollBack returns the computer system to the state it was before the installation began.
UnInstall	UnInstall begins the process to remove an application from the computer. Immediately after UnInstall completes its tasks, RollBack is called.

Let's begin by right-clicking on the Install node and choosing Add Custom Action. You must now select an executable or script file that contains the code we wish to use for this custom action. In our case, the installation code is contained within the IISMon assembly itself. We can choose IISMon by double clicking the Application Folder option and then selecting the IISMon.exe file. Once you have selected the file, click OK and it will be added to our custom actions. When you return to the Custom Actions Editor, you will see a new leaf node in Install.

To instruct our deployment project to use code within our IISMon application to perform the actual service registration, we need only set one property. Ensure that you have the IISMon.exe node selected in the Custom Actions Editor, and then take a look at the Properties window.

Within the Properties window, you will notice a property called InstallerClass. This (oddly enough) tells our deployment project whether the assembly in question contains an Installer class. By setting this property to True, our deployment application will automatically call this class once the file has been placed on the target computer. By calling this class, the application will be registered as a Windows Service.

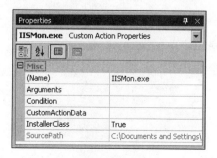

Now we officially have a deployment for our Windows Service application that will copy the required files, and then install the application as a Windows Service. However, we do have one small problem: when the application gets uninstalled, all of the files are removed but the Windows Service database still contains an entry for our application. That is because we didn't tell the installer to remove the service registration if the application is uninstalled. To fix this problem, right-click on the Uninstall node within the Custom Actions Editor and add IISMon.exe just as we did previously. Be sure that the InstallerClass property is set to True when you do this.

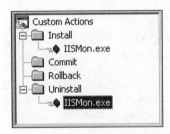

Note that the Commit phase is unused here because it would be an inappropriate place for us to register the Windows Service application. If the install is to commit, all actions so far should have been performed with no errors. If we registered our Windows Service in the Commit phase, the registration might fail, but the setup would still complete successfully. Placing anything within the Rollback phase is unnecessary as well, since rollback reverts the computer back to its state before the application was installed.

That wraps up the deployment project; we can begin testing it now.

Testing the Deployment Project

Testing the deployment project is very simple. If you are going to test this installation on the machine where you created and tested the Windows Service, ensure that the service has been uninstalled and is no longer visible in the Service Control Manager. You may also ensure that the service is no longer installed by using the net start command in a console window, or by checking the Windows Services Database (detailed later in this chapter).

Build the MonInstall project. The Debug directory of the deployment project will now contain five files:

- ❑ InstMsiA.Exe
- ❑ InstMsiW.Exe
- ❑ MonInstall.msi
- ❑ Setup.Exe
- ❑ Setup.Ini

As you can see, among these files are an `.ini` configuration file, a `Setup.exe`, and a Microsoft Installer file. If you intend to test this installation on another computer from that where you built it, you will need to copy across all of these files. When you are ready, run the `Setup.exe` by double-clicking it. You are then greeted with a Welcome screen that contains the name of the application about to be installed, followed by a copyright notice:

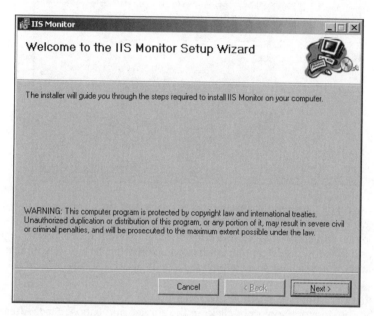

All of the setup dialogs within a Deployment project can be modified. In the above example we have simply chosen to accept the default dialogs.

When the Welcome screen has appeared, click Next. The next window in the setup will ask where the application should be deployed to, and to what level of security should it be deployed: for use by everyone or just the person installing it. By default, the application is copied to `\Program Files\<Author Name>\<Application Name>`. Click Next at this screen.

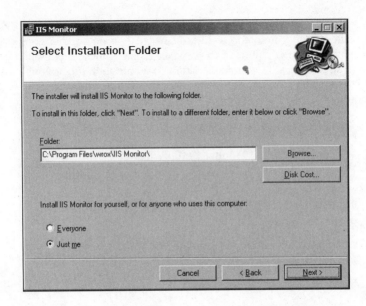

Setup is now ready to begin the installation, so click Next once more.

Once Setup has copied the IISMon assembly, it will take a few seconds to register the assembly as a Windows Service. Once it has completed this task, it will indicate that the application was installed successfully.

To verify that everything went smoothly, open up the Service Control Manager and look for the IIS Monitor. Now right-click on the service and choose Start. After a few seconds the service should start up and the Service Control Manager should change its status to Running. Congratulations – you just created a fully automated distribution package for a Windows Service!

Once you have verified that the service was installed, we must now ensure that it can be removed through the Add/Remove Programs dialog in the control panel. Open this dialog and locate the IIS Monitor application:

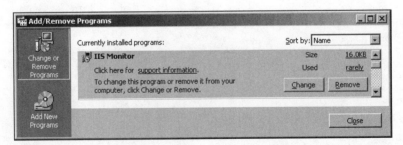

Once you have selected the application, click the Remove button. Once the installation application has removed the IIS Monitor service, look in the Service Control Manager to ensure that it was removed as expected. You'll be happy to know that the installation project has the sense to check the status of the service before it is uninstalled. If the service is running when you attempt to uninstall it, the installation program will stop the service before it continues. Once the service has been stopped, the service will be uninstalled as usual.

Windows Services Database

The Windows Services Database is simply a location in the Windows Registry that contains a list of all the services currently installed, along with a wealth of other information. By viewing the Services Database, you can quickly see where a service is located in the file system, what type of service it is, when the service is to start, and so on.

Let's take a close look at the Windows Services database and explore the information it can provide us.

Exploring the Database

Open the Registry Editor RegEdit.exe, and navigate to the following folder:

HKEY_LOCAL_MACHINE\SYSTEM\CurrentControlSet\Services\

All subkeys of this folder correspond to services. You may notice when viewing this information from RegEdit that there are a lot of services listed that do not appear in the Service Control Manager. The reason for this is that many device drivers are also considered Windows Services, and it is unlikely that a user will ever need to start and stop these services from the Service Control Manager. Each Service listed has a Type key associated with it. If the type happens to be that of a Device Driver, it is omitted from the Service Control Manager.

If you still have the IISMon Service installed from Chapter 3, you should see a subkey listed for it, as shown here:

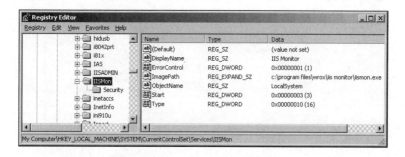

Service Types

Services are generally added by a call to the `CreateService` API; a Win32 UnManaged API. By examining the documentation for this API, we can view the various types a service can be registered as:

Type	Value Data Entry	Description
SERVICE_FILE_SYSTEM_DRIVER	&H2	This Windows Service is classified as a file system driver.
SERVICE_KERNEL_DRIVER	&H1	This Service is classified as a Driver Service.
SERVICE_WIN32_OWN_PROCESS	&H10	This Service runs in its own process.
SERVICE_INTERACTIVE_PROCESS	&H100	This service can interact with the desktop. This type cannot be used by itself and must be used in conjunction with either &H10 or &H20.
SERVICE_WIN32_SHARE_PROCESS	&H20	This Service shares a process.

As you can see, the `IISMon` Windows Service has been installed as a service that runs within its own process, hence the type of hex value 10.

If you attempt to set your service type to that of a device driver or file system driver, you will simply receive an error message at boot time, because your service doesn't implement the required interfaces to qualify as one of these types.

Dependency Information

The Windows Services Database also provides dependency information. This information is the name of a service or services that must be running in order for the particular service to run. In the case of our `IISMon` service, there is no dependency information. So instead scroll down in `RegEdit` until you find the W3SVC service (IIS):

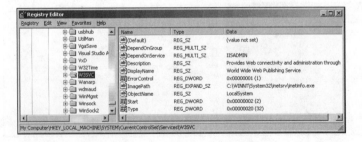

As you can see, IIS requires that the `IISAdmin` service is running before it is allowed to start. Therefore, if you shut down the `IISAdmin` service from within the service control manager, it will also shut down the `W3SVC` service. This dependency information is stored within a multi-string variable. If there were multiple services needed, they would be separated in this list by a hard carriage return.

Programmatic Access

The most obvious and easiest way to access a list of all services within the Service Database is to use the Registry methods within the .NET Framework. These provide you with a quick and efficient way of enumerating the keys contained within the relevant section of the Windows Registry.

> Programmatic access to the Windows Services Database is strongly discouraged unless you simply want to retrieve information. The Service Control Manager must be used whenever changes are needed to this information. If you attempt to change these values in the database without using the appropriate APIs, there is a good chance you will render you PC a thirty-pound paperweight!

To illustrate the use of Registry methods, here is a sample console application called `ListServices` that enumerates all keys within the Windows Service Database, grabbing relevant information from each entry:

```
Imports Microsoft.Win32

Module Module1

    Sub Main()
        Dim hklm As RegistryKey = Registry.LocalMachine
        hklm = hklm.OpenSubKey("SYSTEM\CurrentControlSet\Services", False)

        ' Get all subkeys
        Dim skNames() As String = hklm.GetSubKeyNames
        Dim sk As String
        For Each sk In skNames
            Dim ServiceKey As RegistryKey = Registry.LocalMachine
            ServiceKey = ServiceKey.OpenSubKey( _
                "SYSTEM\CurrentControlSet\Services\" + sk, False)
            Try
                Dim DispName As String = ServiceKey.GetValue("DisplayName")
                Dim ServiceType As Integer = ServiceKey.GetValue("Type")
                If DispName <> "" Then
                    ' Filter out service types.
```

```
            If ServiceType = 16 Then
                Console.WriteLine(DispName)
            End If
        End If
    Catch ex As Exception

    End Try
Next

End Sub

End Module
```

Here we create a `RegistryKey` object to open the Registry to the appropriate location. We then use the `OpenSubKey()` method to get a string array of all subkeys. These subkeys represent all of the services currently installed on the computer. With each subkey name we create a new `RegistryKey` object and open the Registry to that key. Once there we grab two pieces of information: the display name of the service, a string, and an integer value representing the type of service.

With this information we can filter out all the services that are not defined as a `SERVICE_WIN32_OWN_PROCESS` according to the `Type` key. We are then free to print out the `DisplayName` for each of the services that fit our criteria.

There are many APIs that can be used when adding, modifying or viewing the information contained within the database. The most prevalent is the `CreateService` API. The MSDN documentation details this API in depth for those of you that are interested.

Summary

In this chapter you learned to create a deployment project for Window Service applications. You were taught the details necessary to have the installation automatically install and register your service on a target computer. You have also equipped the installation routine with the necessary information to successfully uninstall a Windows Service application should it be necessary.

We then covered the Windows Service database, its location, the information it contains, and how to access that information.

You should now understand enough of Windows Services and how the Windows API deals with them to create most service applications in Visual Basic .NET.

VB.NET

Windows Services

Handbook

Appendix

Support, Errata, and Code Download

We always value hearing from our readers, and we want to know what you think about this book: what you liked, what you didn't like, and what you think we can do better next time. You can send us your comments, either by returning the reply card in the back of the book, or by e-mailing us at feedback@wrox.com. Please be sure to mention the book title in your message. If you have any suggestions about the Handbook series, then you can e-mail the editorial team directly at handbooks@wrox.com. We would love to hear from you with any comments, good or bad.

How to Download the Sample Code for the Book

When you log on to the Wrox site, http://www.wrox.com/, simply locate the title through our Search facility or by using one of the title lists. Click on Download Code on the book's detail page.

The files that are available for download from our site have been archived using WinZip. When you have saved the attachments to a folder on your hard-drive, you will need to extract the files using WinZip, or a compatible tool. Inside the Zip file will be a folder structure and an HTML file that explains the structure and gives you further information, including links to e-mail support, and suggested further reading.

Errata

We've made every effort to ensure that there are no errors in the text or in the code. However, no one is perfect and mistakes can occur. If you find an error in this book, like a spelling mistake or a faulty piece of code, we would be very grateful for feedback. By sending in errata, you may save another reader hours of frustration, and of course, you will be helping us to provide even higher quality information. Simply e-mail the information to support@wrox.com; your information will be checked and if correct, posted to the Errata page for that title.

To find errata, locate this book on the Wrox web site (http://www.wrox.com/ACON11.asp?ISBN=1861007728), and click on the Book Errata link on the book's detail page:

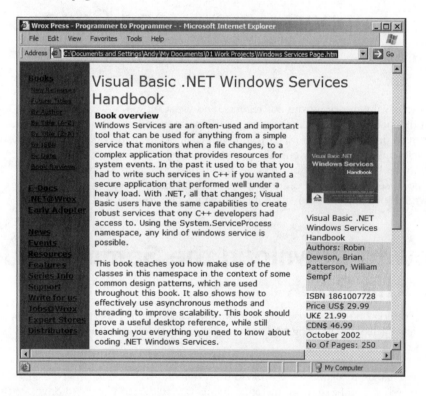

E-Mail Support

If you wish to query a problem in the book with an expert who knows the book in detail then e-mail support@wrox.com, with the title of the book, and the last four numbers of the ISBN in the subject field of the e-mail. A typical e-mail should include the following:

❑ The name, last four digits of the ISBN (in this case 7728), and page number of the problem, in the Subject field

❑ Your name, contact information, and the problem, in the body of the message

We won't send you junk mail. We need the details to save your time and ours. When you send an e-mail message, it will go through the following chain of support:

❑ **Customer Support**

Your message is delivered to our customer support staff. They have files on most frequently asked questions and will answer anything general about the book or the web site immediately.

❑ **Editorial**

More in-depth queries are forwarded to the technical editor responsible for that book. They have experience with the programming language or particular product, and are able to answer detailed technical questions on the subject. Once an issue has been resolved, the editor can post the errata to the web site.

❑ **The Authors**

Finally, in the unlikely event that the editor cannot answer your problem, they will forward the request to the author. We do try to protect the author from any distractions to their writing (or programming); but we are quite happy to forward specific requests to them. All Wrox authors help with the support on their books. They will e-mail the customer and the editor with their response, and again all readers should benefit

The Wrox support process can only offer support for issues that are directly pertinent to the content of our published title. Support for questions that fall outside the scope of normal book support, is provided via our P2P community lists – http://p2p.wrox.com/forum.

p2p.wrox.com

For author and peer discussion, join the P2P mailing lists. Our unique system provides Programmer to Programmer™ contact on mailing lists, forums, and newsgroups, all in addition to our one-to-one e-mail support system. Be confident that the many Wrox authors and other industry experts who are present on our mailing lists are examining any queries posted. At http://p2p.wrox.com/, you will find a number of different lists that will help you, not only while you read this book, but also as you develop your own applications.

To subscribe to a mailing list follow these steps:

- ❏ Go to http://p2p.wrox.com/
- ❏ Choose the appropriate category from the left menu bar
- ❏ Click on the mailing list you wish to join
- ❏ Follow the instructions to subscribe and fill in your e-mail address and password
- ❏ Reply to the confirmation e-mail you receive
- ❏ Use the subscription manager to join more lists and set your mail preferences

VB.NET

Windows Services

Handbook

Index

Index

A Guide to the Index

The index is arranged hierarchically, in alphabetical order, with symbols preceding the letter A. Most second-level entries and many third-level entries also occur as first-level entries. This is to ensure that users will find the information they require however they choose to search for it.

S

Visual Basic .NET Threading Handbook:

Author(s): K. Ardestani, F. C. Ferracchiati, S. Gopikrishna, T. Redkar, S. Sivakumar, T. Titus
ISBN: 1-861007-13-2
US$ 29.99
Can$ 46.99

All .NET languages now have access to the Free Threading Model that many Visual Basic Developers have been waiting for. Compared to the earlier apartment threading model, this gives you much finer control over where to implement threading and what you are given access to. It does also provide several new ways for your application to spin out of control.

This handbook explains how to avoid some common pitfalls when designing multi-threaded applications by presenting some guidelines for good design practice. By investigating .NET's threading model's architecture, you will be able to make sure that your applications take full advantage of it.

What you will learn from this book
- Thread creation
- Using timers to schedule threads to execute at specified intervals
- Synchronizing thread execution - avoiding deadlocks and race conditions
- Spinning threads from within threads, and synchronizing them
- Modelling your applications to a specific thread design model
- Scaling threaded applications by using the ThreadPool class
- Tracing your threaded application's execution in order to debug it

Visual Basic .NET Text Manipulation Handbook:
String Handling and Regular Expressions

Author(s): François Liger, Craig McQueen, Paul Wilton
ISBN: 1-861007-30-2
US$ 29.99
Can$ 46.99

Text forms an integral part of many applications. Earlier version's of Visual
Basic would hide from you the intricacies of how text was being handled,
limiting your ability to control your program's execution or performance. The
.NET Framework gives you much finer control.

This handbook takes an in depth look at the text manipulation classes that
are included within the .NET Framework, in all cases providing you with
invaluable information as to their relative performance merits. The String and
Stringbuilder classes are investigated and the newly acquired support for regular expressions is illustrated in detail.

What you will learn from this book
- String representation and management within the .NET Framework
- Using the StringBuilder object to improve application performance
- Choosing between the different object's methods when manipulating text
- How to safely convert between String and other data types
- How to take advantage of .NET's Unicode representation of text for
  Internationalization
- The use of regular expressions including syntax and pattern matching to
  optimize your text manipulation operations

Visual Basic .NET Class Design Handbook:
Coding Effective Classes

Visual Basic .NET Class Design Handbook: Coding Effective Classes

Author(s): Andy Olsen, Damon Allison, James Speer
ISBN: 1-861007-08-6
US$ 29.99
Can$ 46.99

Designing effective classes that you do not need to revisit and revise over and over again is an art. Within the .NET Framework, whatever code you write in Visual Basic .NET is encapsulated within the class hierarchy of the .NET Framework.

By investigating in depth the various members a class can contain, this handbook aims to give you a deep understanding of the implications of all the decisions you can make at design time. This book will equip you with the necessary knowledge to build classes that are robust, flexible, and reusable.

- **What you will learn from this book**
- The role of types in .NET
- The different kinds of type we can create in VB.NET
- How VB.NET defines type members
- The fundamental role of methods as containers of program logic
- The role of constructors and their effective use
- Object cleanup and disposal
- When and how to use properties and indexers to encapsulate data
- How .NET's event system works
- How to control and exploit inheritance in our types
- The logical and physical code organisation through namespaces and assemblies